THE PURSUIT OF

IDENTITY

&

PURPOSE

THE PURSUIT OF

IDENTITY

&

PURPOSE

CREATING TRUE HAPPINESS AND DIRECTION THROUGH A JOURNEY OF SELF DISCOVERY

CHARLES BROWNE

The Pursuit of Identity & Purpose © Copyright 2021 Charles Browne

For more information, email me@therealcharlesbrowne.com

ISBN: 979-8-9855062-0-4

JOIN THE FACEBOOK GROUP!

Don't go it alone!

Join one of the most engaged and helpful groups on Facebook by scanning the code above, or you can search "Pursuit of Identity & Purpose" from your Facebook account.

To get the best experience from this book, I've found readers who join and engage in the Facebook community are able to implement faster and take the steps needed to overcome the fear and obstacles that hold them back.

You can get in touch with me by visiting:
www.therealcharlesbrowne.com

To my children, who both inspire my journey and give me the strength to keep walking.

TABLE OF CONTENTS

TESTIMONIALS

Here's what some of my clients have to say about my Identity & Purpose framework:

I am separated from my partner in a very peaceful, respectful, and amicable way, I am pursuing my purpose, changing careers and completing my college degree. 3 months working with Charles completely changed my life.

I think just making it through the day with a smile on my face says it all - not sure where I'd be on my own, but I know I was in a pretty dark place before I met Charles. Things are getting better, and I owe so much of my progress to him and his coaching and guidance.

One of the great things about working with Charles is that, first, I believe and trust that he's authentically invested in my growth and development. Additionally, he has lived the experience that provides credibility and valuable perspective to the advice and guidance he imparts.

I am a strong believer in therapy and recommend it often, but a coach can say things to you that a therapist can't. If you have a mental illness, by all means see a therapist, or psychiatrist; otherwise, a great coach like Charles will get you farther faster than therapy.

Charles helped me get back to basics, to reacquaint myself with my needs and values, and to align my decision-making with meeting those needs and values. He has helped me identify where - and more importantly, WHY - I've strayed from my true self, and guided me back toward better alignment. He's there for me in ways I didn't know I needed, and I really appreciate his care, concern, and even the "tough love!"

Charles' insights have been invaluable because he has helped me with both my personal life and my business. I look forward to our conversations because he keeps me accountable to my goals. Being self-employed, it is priceless to have someone to keep me accountable and on track.

Charles is a mentor and friend that can help you learn about how to identify and live by your personal values and needs in a way that can transform and improve how you feel about yourself and how you relate to others.

Charlie is great at working with people of all ages to help them become the best version of themselves. He helped me get through a difficult breakup and gave me the skills to meet my own need rather than relying on someone else to meet my needs for me. I can confidently say I am a better and happier person after working with Charlie.

Get with Charles and get some clarity.

(Identities withheld to respect their privacy)

INTRODUCTION

"Charles? Well? What problem do you solve? Who do you want your business to serve?"

"Uhhhh, I help people with problems, and I solve the problems people have."

"That's not an answer. You have to know who you help and how or I can't help you. What do you want?"

This wasn't the first time I'd struggled to define myself, my service, my value to the world. Betsy was just the latest in a long line of people who had recognized great potential in me and was trying desperately to get me to commit to a market, an industry, anything to help her help me carve out my niche in the world. And like the scores before her, she was powerless to do so without my declaration of who I was, what I wanted, and why I mattered.

What she and the others before her didn't know is that I grew up in a household where identity and individuality were not only uncomfortable, they were discouraged. Not rocking the boat and not calling attention to myself was the order of the day. It's not that my parents were purposely abusive or intentionally neglectful; it's just that things went much more smoothly when their needs were allowed to be the center of attention, and I went along with the crowd.

And it was the root of all my problems.

As I wouldn't learn until much later in life, it was this dynamic that had molded me into the emotional chameleon I had come to value so much. People pleasing, accommodating, going with the flow...call it what you will, but my survival hinged on my ability to suppress my own identity and needs in order to keep the peace and not be a burden.

That technique which had served me so well in childhood had now, in my late 40s, created a full-blown identity crisis. But it was even worse. The few things I had in my life that gave me direction and identity had been taken away almost simultaneously. My second marriage was ending and my six-figure management position with a Fortune-100 company had been eliminated. All I had left was that I was still "father" to my two children, but what kind of father could I be without a job and a strained relationship with their mother?

There were huge voids in my identity and I was becoming unraveled.

I had spent my life searching for the holy grail of self-help. I read books, downloaded tools, created dream boards, and covered my mirror with sticky note affirmations. Nothing seemed to help. It all made sense, don't get me wrong, but none of it really made a difference. I was still shrouded in doubt and felt like I was chasing the next thing that was supposed to help my life make sense and have a purpose. None of it did.

Throughout all that reading though, one word, one concept felt like the sexiest, most amazing thing I had ever heard: authenticity. To only have one voice, one identity, one persona guiding and driving your choices. It seemed like a fantasy at the time, but I was drawn to the idea of being a singular person of integrity and value. Oh man, what it must feel like to know exactly how you're going to respond in any given scenario.

I did not. There were too many variables to know what I'd say or do. Who's asking? Who's listening? What is everybody else doing? Where are we? Is it raining? My reactions to any given situation were just that—reactions. Momentary emotional responses to a plethora of outside influences. Constantly working to minimize my risk and avoid confrontation or being "found out."

But still, somehow I felt that if I could figure out this whole "authenticity" thing, there might just be some peace and quiet and focus in my life. I had to try, it was a compulsion.

I knew I was being heavily influenced by that childhood I mentioned. I am an adult child of an alcoholic, an adult child of a sexual, mental, and physical abuse survivor, so I started there. Professionally speaking, root cause analysis is part of my job, so I started digging into the root of what made me "me."

Now, don't get me wrong, there are obviously a lot of terrific books and blogs out there, but the *vast* majority didn't provide much assistance. They seemed to have been written with keywords in mind, not to provide actual help. At least not much actionable help. I learned a lot, even some tactics (we'll talk about this concept more later), but the more I learned the more I realized that all this advice was focused on addressing the effects and not the cause.

Or worse, they completely ignored the context of my life and personality and obstacles.

For example, books about goals. Do you know why you're not achieving your goals, or why it's so hard to accomplish a goal? Because it's probably not *your* goal. It's perhaps your Mom's goal for you, or your boss's goal for you, or society's goal for you and if you're honest with yourself, you'd realize you don't have any trouble achieving your goals (polished off that whole pizza by yourself didn't you?), but you do have trouble completing *other* peoples' goals.

So the issue wasn't my capability to accomplish things, but my willingness to accomplish things. Limiting beliefs, confirmation biases, self-fulfilling prophecies all conspired to keep me right where I was, content with not having needs or an identity.

In *The Matrix* when Neo first meets the Oracle she draws his attention to a plaque over her door that reads, "Temet nosce"— know thyself. All my problems, all my successes had only one thing in common: me. I felt that the more I learned about myself the less I would have to choose or decide and the more authentic I would become. I reread a lot of books with this in mind.

The problem, as I've already asserted, was that all those books only addressed one issue and focused on alleviating the effects, but not the cause, of that specific issue. It's like wanting to lose some weight so you buy a program to make your forearms thinner, then another to make your thighs thinner, then another to burn fat from your back. It sounds ridiculous when I say it that way, but that was my experience with self-help materials: each presented only a piece of the puzzle and did not acknowledge the systemic problem at hand.

Along my journey, I came to realize that what all these seemingly separate issues had in common was my choices, my decision-making process, and my motivations for those decisions. Basically, I believe our lives are the accumulation of our choices, and if our decision-making process is tainted by external factors we'll never make a choice that is authentic to us.

More troubling is that a life led by that decision-making process becomes unrecognizable to us. "Why did I move here?" "Why oh why did I ever take this job?" "Why am I not happy?" "What problem do I solve?" "Who do I want my business to serve?"

So, I set out to make more congruent choices, but there was only one problem: in the absence of external influence, what was left? If I'm not making choices to please others or to win acceptance and approval, then what motivates my choices? Hmmmmm.

What is the universal set of standards by which we each navigate life? How do we know what is important to us? How do we know how to act and choose? Where do we discover our "why" that everybody is always going on about?

I figured that each of these self-help strategies and categories had at least part of the answer.

I found my answer in the combination and interplay between values, emotional needs, and self-care. In my experience, they create the Pyramid of Fulfillment.

During my studies, I would write my insights and observations on the last page of my journal. I considered the last page of my journal the home for the key takeaways of each lesson or book I was reading at the time. I would often flip to that page randomly when I was thinking about something or searching for answers, hoping the answer would be there. Then one day it was, and my life changed!

While staring at that page of my values, emotional needs, quotes, and beliefs I had a moment where I disconnected from them and thought, "Wow, this is a good dude. I wish I knew this guy. I wish I could be friends with this guy. He seems cool. He seems like he'd be fun to hang around and talk with...I think we would be great friends. Oh shit....…that's me! I'm that person! I like that person! I love that person! *I'm never not going to be that person again!*"

What I had discovered at that moment was my true identity. I realized that any other version of myself was in violation of who that guy was/is and was a betrayal to him. I cried...a little at first, then a lot.

From that moment forward I have striven to make choices that are in complete alignment with who that person is, what he believes, what he needs and wants, what he values in life, and I've been happier, more focused, and more energetic ever since. It wasn't without its challenges and setbacks, but every day has been better since I discovered my Identity & Purpose.

It didn't take long for those around me to take notice either. Soon, as the reborn often do, I became a zealot spreading the word and worth of knowing your Identity & Purpose and using them to guide your choices in life. And not long after that, I started coaching others to realign their lives as well with great success.

> *Charles helped me get back to basics, to reacquaint myself with my needs and values, and to align my decision-making with meeting those needs and values. He has helped me identify where—and more impor-tantly, why—I've strayed from my true self, and guided me back toward better alignment. He's there for me in ways I didn't know I needed, and I really appreciate his care, concern, and even the "tough love"!*

But utilizing this knowledge to make decisions was just the first step of living a life of fulfillment. I learned that if values define "what" is important, it's our emotional needs that define "how" we go about living them.

In the months and years that followed that epiphany, I've created an ever-expanding framework that has guided my decision-making ever since. I've also shared it with hundreds of friends and clients, none of whom are ever the same afterward. But here's the really cool part: none of them had to learn a new language, or force themselves to do anything awkward either.

If we know anything about happiness we know that it's not the accumulation of things, but the removal and avoidance of stresses and compromises. The framework I'm going to share with you in this book is not a means to pile more requirements and stress onto your already exhausted psyche, but to help you ethically and unashamedly remove violations from your life to live in alignment with your true identity, to realize your true purpose.

We're going to talk about all the ways I learned to love and forgive my past mistakes, celebrate my failures and embrace my true identity. My hope is that you'll continue reading and follow the path I've laid out for you to fuel your own Pursuit of Identity & Purpose.

SECTION I

Assessment

CHAPTER 1

VALUES

"It's not hard to make decisions when you know what your values are."

—Roy Disney

THE VALUE SYSTEM & ITS PLACE IN SOCIETY

The first step in the journey of discovering your true identity and purpose is to determine what matters to you, what really matters to you. In the absence of all other influences (like making your Mom happy or answering other peoples' needs) what is your code of conduct?

I often ask my clients to play the Powerball/Castaway game. In it, you pretend you've just won the $1B Powerball jackpot or you're stranded on a deserted island (or you've just won the $1B Powerball jackpot or you've bought a deserted island!). In each scenario, you can free yourself from other peoples' judgments, wants, needs, and expectations for you and your life.

Who would you be? What would you do with your time and

energy? How would you live out the remainder of your days? More importantly, what wouldn't you do? Most of us can't answer this question.

As a society, we have created a set of rules and ethics that we try to abide by. We know those rules as morals. These morals are often established through external forces such as religion, culture, or experience. However, not everyone has the same morals. This is why some people may think that what is considered morally wrong or bad by others can be morally right or good.

We all have our own morals and ethics that we follow in order to make up a set of personal values. Morals are the things that we believe are right or wrong; ethics are the principles of conduct regarding the rightness or wrongness of certain behaviors.

Values are important because they help us to make decisions, be true to ourselves, and live a meaningful life. Values are our guiding principles in life. They are what we believe in and what motivate us. A personal value is something that you believe in, for example how you want to live your life. It's something that guides every decision you make.

The function of values is to help us become more aware of who we are and who we want to be in the future. Values give meaning to our lives because they tell us how we want our lives to be lived. The priority of our values can also evolve over time and change based on the context of the situation.

In order to change your value system for the better, you have to know what values you hold. Finding this out is a difficult task because most of us don't even think about our values until we are in a situation where they matter. To help you through this process, here are some self-exploration exercises that will help you identify your values and how they affect your life.

EXERCISE 1

Imagine yourself in an ideal world where all of your needs are fulfilled without difficulty or strain. What would your life look like? What would be important to you? Create an "ideal day" for yourself where every-thing goes according to plan; what does that day look like? What do you do during the productive and nonproductive times?

We've been conditioned our entire lives to make our decisions through the lens of how it affects those around us. How will our choices please or disappoint those around us? If you grew up in a household where your needs were not met in a timely or judicious manner (because you were raised by an addict or a narcissist), you're especially susceptible to suppressing your own wants and needs.

Now, I'm not an idiot, I understand that we live in a society. A society with rules and responsibilities, so I'm not suggesting that my prescription for living your Identity & Purpose is to simply cast aside everyone and everything and live like a billionaire stranded on a remote island somewhere.

But, just for a moment, imagine what it would feel like to make all your decisions in a really selfish way. When I played this game for the first time it was both liberating and shocking. I realized that I did a *lot* of things for other people in an attempt to win their favor or make them happy.

The difference between my actual choices and my Powerball choices was that my Powerball choices were free from fear...they were authentic to who I wanted to be, not who I thought I needed to be in order to be accepted.

I realized that my actual decisions and choices, though, were like a leaf in the wind, getting blown about by seemingly random forces. One minute I was rueing a job that was sucking the very marrow from my soul, the next I was applying for a promotion in that same company because who wouldn't want a promotion? People who get promotions are cool and important and likable, right?

It was this dynamic that had created a life I didn't recognize let alone want. But, if I didn't want a promotion what did I want? What did I value?

In ethics, value denotes assigning a degree of importance to a thing or action, with the aim of determining what actions are best to do or what way is best to live, or to describe the significance of different actions. In the pursuit of Identity & Purpose, values are our guideposts, they define what's important to us, but most of us are unaware of what our values actually are.

When I started my journey of self-discovery I honestly wasn't sure where to start. I often use the analogy that we are in the eye of our own hurricane, all of life's demands and influences swirling around us, chaotic and noisy, and every once in a while bonking us in the head.

But with all that "stuff" flying by, how do we know which stuff is important and which is just trash? What we really need is to understand what we would do or choose in the absence of all that influence.

EXERCISE 2

The process for determining your values is fairly simple. I suggest starting with a fairly comprehensive (big) list of values. Be sure the list isn't organized in any manner that would suggest the values have any specific hierarchy or, well, value. I arrange my list alphabetically to avoid the suggestion of bias.

Write or mark every value that has meaning to you, any value that resonates with you, or any value that you admire.

One of the reasons this exercise is so powerful is because you can't cheat. There are no right or wrong values. I challenge you to find a value that is "bad." This is going to be very important later in your assessment of your identity, but we'll talk about that when we get there.

VALUES EXERCISE:
therealcharlesbrowne.com/resources

Once you've marked every value that has meaning to you go back through the list and select your top 10-12 values.

Finally, and I know this can be tough, select your top 3-5 nonnegotiable personal values.

Boom! You've done it!

Now create an acronym or write them down or do whatever you have to do to be able to recall them from memory.

These are the values that guide your very essence and, if you think about it for a minute, are the values that were violated each and every time something in your life went bad or was just "off" (like a job, relationship, etc.).

Use these values as a compass for each decision you make going forward. Given any number of options, one of those options will be more in alignment with your values than the others—that's the best choice for you.

EXERCISE 3

More importantly than which values you choose is what you do with them after you've selected your personal values. To be fair, a list of values is useless until they're put into the context of our lives. To do that you must define those words for yourself.

Don't just paste in Webster's definition, write your own definition of that value. For example, I guarantee that you and I have *very* different definitions of adventure. Be sure that you are crystal clear on what a particular value means to you personally as you move forward.

For example, just because you and I both chose adventure as a top 5 nonnegotiable value doesn't mean we both live that value in the same way. As a Navy veteran and martial artist, my idea of adventure may be very different from yours.

What's important is that you understand and accept what that value means to you and how you want to express it. Do not accept anyone else's definition of that value except your own. This is how we got into trouble in the first place.

> **PRO TIP: YES! You can redo this exercise again and again as you learn more about yourself and revise what you believe are your top values.**

We'll discuss potential challenges with this exercise in the final section of the book, but for now, take a breath, don't overthink it, and celebrate this step. To help you keep your values organized you may download my Values Worksheet from the link below or create something similar for yourself.

VALUES WORKSHEET:
therealcharlesbrowne.com/resources

The only test or validation that you need to perform right now is to reflect on the selected values and ask yourself if they "feel" right. Again, there are no *bad* values, so you should be happy and proud of your selections. Congratulations.

—————————   **EXERCISE 4**   —————————

The final exercise related to your values relates to Columns 3 and 4 of the worksheet. If you haven't downloaded the worksheet, Columns 3 and 4 ask you to reflect on ways that your current life honors or violates those top 3-5 nonnegotiable values. Understanding these major contributors is a very important step in realigning your life to be more in alignment with those values.

Obviously, things, people, or situations that violate our values are contributing to our anxiety and stress. Things that align with those values are a source of joy and fulfillment. In a perfect world, we would have no violations and live in a perpetual state of values alignment.

Your values are the foundation of your identity and contribute heavily to your purpose, so above all else be honest with yourself about their selection. When in doubt in the future, use these values to guide your decisions and choices.

Though the priority of your values may change throughout your life or following significant life events, your belief in their value will not. If you believe honesty is an important value, you will always believe honesty is an important value so avoid suppressing or compromising that value as much as possible.

In the next chapter, we'll start to explore how to express each of these values in a way that meets our emotional needs in order to build a life we can be proud of.

CHAPTER 2

Emotional Needs

"You aren't alive if you aren't in need."

— Henry Cloud

Values are great. They are the expression of what is important to us and the basis of our identity. Faith, entrepreneurialism, charity, wealth...but it doesn't really matter what your values are if you don't pursue them in a way that feeds your soul.

While I evaluated my own values exercise results, I struggled with what to do with this newfound insight.

If our values help us define what is important to us, our emotional needs help us understand how to achieve them. In the search for our true identity, knowing what we value is definitely an important step, but how we put those values into practice is the true game-changer for creating a life of fulfillment and joy. Ensuring that your emotional needs are met is what will allow you to transition from reactive decision-maker (being influenced by external sources) to proactive decision-maker (making choices that align with the life we want to design).

Our emotional needs are at play 24/7/365 influencing our choices and behaviors on a subconscious level. And because of that, they are at the root of all our dysfunctional behavior. The drive to meet our emotional needs is so strong that, if properly harnessed, it can be the driving force behind all the positive change you want in life, too. They're also the key to understanding why we do what we do.

Don't believe me?

> *When I first met Adam he was accepting of the things that were outside of his control. He allowed his boss to change his performance expectations often and didn't think he minded when he had to change his vacation plans at the last minute. It was just the way things were, and who was he to complain or push back?*

> *Once he read, understood, and ranked his emotional needs he came to understand that all of that uncertainty was actually causing him a lot of stress and overall dissatisfaction. Uncertainty was actually one of his least favorable emotional needs. The constant lack of consistency was keeping him in a state of fear and gave him little hope for his future.*

> *But because Adam had grown up in a household with little consistency and certainty he was used to it and convinced himself that that's what it meant to be an employee. He assumed any dissatisfaction*

he was feeling was his problem, not a reaction to a misalignment of his needs.

Once Adam recognized how detrimental the constant uncertainty was to his emotional state and how important contribution is (his top emotional need) he was able to have an open conversation with his boss and the other people in his life and let them know that he needs more consistency and notice to be happy.

Accepting that he would thrive much better in an environment that allowed him to organize according to his strengths allowed Adam and his boss to have an open discussion about how just a few simple changes would help him contribute at a higher level resulting in a win-win for him and the company.

Adam's newfound peace made a significant impact on his morale and in turn, on his performance. Additionally, he has applied this awareness to all aspects of his life and he's comfortable letting his friends and family know that he's more comfortable knowing their plans ahead of time and he's happiest when he's able to contribute to the group by helping plan and organize their activities.

Adam's experience isn't a fluke, but it also didn't happen overnight. This book and its lessons are about making small changes that are for your benefit without pissing everyone around you off. His story is an example of how being a better version of yourself is in everyone's best interest.

Since we are born with these needs, our views and ideas around our self-worth and beliefs were heavily influenced by how consistently and promptly those needs were met. If you were born into a dysfunctional household (and who wasn't?) your young mind made associations and comparisons based on your caregiver's response to your needs. When they ignored or berated your requests you interpreted that to mean that your needs were not important, that you were not important to them, and you sought to meet those needs elsewhere, often in less than healthy or productive ways.

When I first began my self-improvement journey I knew that my parents' addiction and trauma had affected me at an early age, but I didn't know in just what ways. I struggled with low self-esteem and insecurity which led me to constantly seek approval by lying and exaggerating. Despite countless attempts, including hanging signs on my bedroom door that said, "Don't Lie," I could not fight the unconscious compulsion to always paint a rosier picture even if it meant deceiving people. That behavior led to feelings of shame and confirmation bias that perpetuated the cycle of not feeling "good enough," leading to further exaggerations and embellishments.

EXERCISE 5

Reflect on the things that you are ashamed of or just don't like about yourself. And I'm not talking about your

thighs or unibrow. But instead of feeling ashamed of
them, ask why you may have done them. What need
do you think you were trying to meet?

But that's not to say we're all being influenced equally or by the same needs. To better understand how to harness the power of these unceasing needs toward a purposeful life we need to first know what they are. For myself and my clients I use the Six Basic Human Emotional Needs model popularized by Tony Robbins. They are, listed alphabetically:

1. **Certainty** - a sense of security, predictability, safety, and comfort (Personality)
2. **Contribution -** the desire to give to others or as a member of a team through acts of service (Spirituality)
3. **Growth/Knowledge** - a desire to learn and evolve in capacity, capability, and knowledge (Spirituality)
4. **Love & Connection** - a sense of acceptance, belonging, and support with someone or something (Personality)
5. **Significance -** a sense of uniqueness, individuality, and being special (Personality)
6. **Uncertainty** - a sense of change, interest, and the unknown (Personality)

Certainty - this need requires that you feel safe and assured about the future which is typically accomplished by avoiding change, new situations, and new people. Since this is almost impossible (even Tom Hanks eventually got rescued from that island) you will frequently adjust your expectations and standards in order to convince yourself you're in control. Obviously, if left unchecked you will talk yourself out of every good idea you ever have and could develop addictive or obsessive tendencies.

Contribution - this need is the driving force behind giving. Contribution-focused people need everything they do to have meaning and purpose. Although this can be the motivation behind making a profound difference in the world, it can also lead to burnout and neglect of self and those closest to you. The key to ensuring you're not being taken advantage of is choosing a cause near and dear to your heart.

Growth/Knowledge - this need pushes us to continually strive to become a better version of ourselves. Through education, advancement, and experience we are driven toward mastery and perfection. If this need dominates your behavior you will often move on to new experiences and relationships in pursuit of something better (often confused with uncertainty). To keep this in check, growth-driven individuals need to cultivate an internal questioning attitude that challenges their own beliefs and emotional intelligence.

Love & Connection - this need is punctuated by the longing for and constant pursuit of deep, meaningful relationships with someone or something (like an organization or cause). Connection seekers have numerous social ties which can lead to a loss of self and neglect of all else trying to maintain them all.

Significance - this need requires recognition (in any of its many forms) to be fulfilled. In general, this need compels you to be seen, heard, and valued by your internal measure of what makes you unique (compliments on your height aren't going to do it). Significance is achieved through relative measures, meaning significance can be achieved by raising ourselves up or by pulling others down.

Uncertainty - this need is driven by change and variety. Though quite common, not all uncertainty is adrenaline-based. Some peoples' need for uncertainty is achieved through frequent career, relationships, or environmental changes. Though most uncertainty driven people have a high risk tolerance they can also be reckless and not amass much of a nest egg or strong personal ties.

The key to using these needs to understand your motives and how your needs are affecting you is to understand that, even though we all share these same basic needs, their hierarchy and ratio are as unique to you as your fingerprints.

Yes, we all need to have a life and experiences that fulfill each of these needs, but what is most important to you and what their individual contributions to your overall emotional health are is an answer only you can provide.

EXERCISE 6

To get a handle on this, at least initially, go back and re-read those needs and rank them from 1-6 (most important to least important to you). That's the first step in personalizing these needs. As you can see, just by ranking them in order of importance you have chosen a combination that is 1 in 46,656!

Now, the next step, which is even more nuanced, would be to assign a percentage value to each need. That is to say, they're not weighted equally in your mind. Just because there are six needs doesn't mean that each is worth 16.666667% of your emotional wellness.

In fact, I argue that your top two needs (the ones you ranked #1 and #2 above) account for 51% of your total emotional needs makeup. But, it's not really important to know exactly how much each need is influencing you, what is important to believe is that:

1. Your top two needs are the majority stakeholders in your mind
2. *All* your needs need some level of satisfaction (imagine buckets of differing sizes)

When our life choices don't create an environment that fulfills our emotional needs in a meaningful way, our subconscious will work to fulfill our needs in a convenient way. If your dominant needs have been neglected or ignored you're likely feeling disappointed, frustrated, or just out of sync with what's going on around you and you're starting to take notice of unhealthy or self-destructive patterns.

Emotional needs are not just about fulfilling our basic needs. They are also about creating an environment that fulfills our emotional needs in a meaningful way so that our subconscious will be happy with the environment and take it as a safe place to live.

Research has shown that even if people consciously don't like their living environments, they subconsciously feel at home; this is because they unconsciously identify the place as their safe haven out of familiarity, not approval.

As with the values exercise, there are no right or wrong needs. There is no better or worse order or ratio. What's most important is, as always, that you're honest with yourself first so you can be more honest about your needs to others and live in a way that is healthy for you.

The Pursuit of Identity & Purpose is about shedding false identities and expectations, not because we want the world to revolve around us, but because in order to be of service to others we need to be the best versions of ourselves.

Which brings us to our next topic. With these two anchors, values and needs, we now have the basis to define our true selves.

CHAPTER 3

Identity

"Be yourself; everyone else is already taken."

— Oscar Wilde

Believe it or not, in Chapters 1 & 2 you learned the cornerstones of what makes up the discovery of your identity. You've learned more about yourself in that short time than most people learn in a lifetime. Not because the concepts are difficult or overly complicated, but because of the simple fact that we're not taught to take time to define ourselves.

When I was struggling to discover myself I was devouring books, lectures, and advice as quickly as I could. Each new concept or consideration nudged me forward, but there was never anything that I would consider a lightning bolt. Until there was.

As I was consuming all these ideas I kept a journal, more of a notebook really. In it, I would jot down ideas, quotes, and questions that went unanswered. On the last page of that notebook though, were the takeaways (from several sources) about my values and needs.

I had done the exercises from a few different lessons and I had (instinctively?) collected these few traits and tendencies in one, centralized place. Anything that I thought gave an insight into a character or personality trait went on that page.

One day, quite unexpectedly, I was staring at the various scribbles. There were my top nonnegotiable personal values, my emotional needs, and a smattering of other "things" about myself. And as I looked at that page something shifted inside me and I became detached from the writings. I began to see them, not as a description of me, but as the description of someone, anyone, and it hit me: this was (in the absence of my shame and self-limiting beliefs) a good person.

There wasn't one bad value or selfish need. Not one ugly habit or shortcoming and I realized that if I could live in alignment with those values and needs, I too would be a good person. The next realization was more subtle but equally as important: this had been the real me all along.

The dissatisfaction and stress I had been feeling, the low self-esteem, the distraction and confusion, the acting out, and the self-sabotage were my subconscious way of rebelling against the personas I had been living as versus living in my authentic self.

One of the skills that has allowed our species to progress so rapidly from one generation to the next is our ability to communicate and pass down our knowledge. And, as powerful as that is, it's not without its risks. Learning a certain skill at age seven when it took your grandparent 48 years to learn that same expertise allows you to focus on acquiring and refining new knowledge. Thriving, not just surviving.

The catch is...what if that information they passed along was wrong, incomplete, or based on faulty assumptions?

The risk is that passing down knowledge and *blindly accepting* it exposes future generations to the same risks and pitfalls over and over and over. (Like *The Matrix*!) In the physical world, this is usually corrected pretty quickly.

The noisy nope-rope lizards bite!

But the emotional and psychological lessons are harder to learn because their associations are harder to make. We don't realize that we lie and exaggerate to try to create acceptance and thereby fulfill our emotional needs. Our brains are hardwired to make associations instead of having to analyze every single thing we encounter. In your brain, if you see a zebra you assess it at the same threat level as a horse without having to think about it too much—close enough.

This is a survival mechanism that conserves calories and keeps us alive longer. The less processing the brain has to do the more energy and attention is available for more important decisions (that might involve life-threatening situations).

So, with our brain using shortcuts as often as possible, applying inherited beliefs and values, and the connection between the emotional and physical worlds being fuzzy at best, we're doomed to live in a way that isn't congruent with our true selves.

Each one of us, regardless of our current challenges, has had moments in our lives that have resulted in a very strong physical or emotional response. In some instances, we were feeling powerful, optimistic, and, however briefly, invincible. We've also experienced situations that created a response that was extremely uncomfortable and caused us to invoke a survival response (fight, flight, or freeze). Regardless of whether they were positive or negative, they were the physical manifestation of our values being directly honored or violated. I call those Zone Moments.

These moments are powerful insights into our authentic selves. They are situations in which our values and needs are either being fully realized and honored, or directly assaulted and violated. These moments are extremely valuable on our journey to self-discovery because whether they were positive or negative we can deconstruct them and either leverage (for the good moments) or avoid (for the bad ones) similar environments.

───────── **EXERCISE 7** ─────────

Think back to a particularly amazing or troubling experience in your past. Maybe you reached a boiling point and blew up at a co-worker or family member. Maybe you found yourself in a new role and were so comfortable and effective that everyone remarked on how well you handled the situation.

Regardless of whether it was a positive or negative experience capture as much detail as you can and try to determine which of your values was being violated or honored. Odds are if it's a significant moment in your mind, more than one value was involved.

Now, consider your role in the event and consider how you responded. Again, whether it was positive or negative try to understand which of your needs was being met or denied.

Knowing the elements of a Zone Moment means you can avoid similar situations in the future by establishing healthy boundaries or recreate those conditions just by the choices you make.

In a perfect world, we would make decisions and choices that completely aligned with our values in a way that met all of our emotional needs all day, every day. But I'm not an idiot. I know we live in a society and we have responsibilities; we can't just stop paying rent because it "doesn't align with my core values."

The goal of this book and my practice, though, is to empower each of us to make better decisions that do align with our authentic identity and by doing so create a life that is fulfilling and, dare I say, happy!

The concept is pretty simple: things that honor our values and fulfill our needs give us a better sense of happiness. Things that directly violate our values or deplete our emotional needs make us, well, less happy.

I'm not going to challenge Shawn Achor on theories around happiness, but it has been my observation and experience that the more aligned I am to my values and the more I am able to fulfill my own emotional needs, the happier and more fulfilled I am. Put simply:

$$Happiness = Honors - Violations$$

If identity is as simple as knowing our values and needs, why aren't we all 100% authentic creatures? The short answer is...lots of reasons.

First, we have two very powerful drives influencing us nearly constantly and they're rooted in our survival instinct which, as you may have heard, is notoriously difficult to override. The first compulsion within us is to be a member of a group. As cooperative mammals, we are predisposed to seek the safety and prosperity of a larger group.

Groups, as a rule, tend to fare better than individuals where survival and safety are concerned. Cooperative behaviors leverage the accomplishments of a few to benefit the many. The most obvious example is a small hunting party bringing back enough food to feed the entire tribe.

Prehistorically speaking, the first groups of us were formed to gain access to or protect vital resources, like water and shelter. We huddled together and kept each other warm and our united front or scattering retreats confused predators, improving our combined and individual odds of survival. Because of this, our ancestors were born into their groups (tribes) or assimilated into other groups through "marriage" or acquired membership in myriad shady ways, I'm sure.

The point is, being a member of a group didn't take much thought or effort back then. You were a part of a group or you were probably dead. Even today, you're born into a group (even if it's just two of you) and it begins influencing you on day one. As our societies have grown and become more sophisticated, though, becoming a member of a new group isn't as easy as having a welcoming smile and cheery demeanor. We need to be able to contribute to that group's goals or purpose.

Here comes the threat to our individuality and authenticity. To be welcomed into a group we are accepting that we will have to cooperate, we will have to compromise, for the greater good. So, this is the first assault on our authentic selves. We're taught, from a very early age, to "behave"—to abide by the group's rules and standards—and we do it, willingly, because of our instinct to survive.

The second compulsion within us is, once we are accepted into a group, we're driven to attain status within that group. Higher status means better or more resources. Better cuts of meat, safer sleeping arrangements, better mating choices. Again, these are primal and are tied directly to our instinctual drive to survive and propagate.

How that affects our authenticity is that, unless you created the group, the group has its own definitions of success, value, and "appropriate" behavior. Only members who emulate those values ascend the social ladder. So, again, we are instinctively driven to suppress our individuality to increase our odds of staying alive and enjoying whatever level of comfort and security the group can provide.

Of course, things have changed a bit from the picture I paint above. Our modern groups are much more nuanced and specialized. In fact, we are each a member of dozens of groups. Professional groups, religious groups, social groups, socioeconomic groups, brand groups, sports groups...the list goes on and on.

Now imagine that each and every one of those groups is acting to modify and control your behavior. It's overwhelming and we're constantly changing hats to gain or protect our status within those individual groups. Actions that are not in accordance with the group's standards and expectations can threaten our status and even membership in the group in which we are instinctively fighting to remain.

Say something bad about a coach or quarterback and you are ostracized from the group, no longer welcome in physical or virtual gatherings. The same is true when you question a family member's political or religious decisions or comments.

These influences create an environment where we constantly have to police ourselves to protect our membership and status within society. In some cases, it can be very positive, like when we band together and decide that violence against another group is no longer to be tolerated. But it can work equally powerfully in the opposite direction as well, causing us to violate our values.

It's the violation of our values and denial of our emotional needs that causes that inexplicable tension and even anger within us. It is more important than ever for our individual values and beliefs to guide our choices and actions, which is why I am thrilled you're still reading this book!

We'll talk more about rectifying the conflict between being an individual (the only path to true acceptance and happiness) and being accepted by various groups (the instinct to survive) a little later in the book. But first, we're going to continue to define our authentic selves and worry about cleaning up the self-sabotage and objections later.

CHAPTER 4

Purpose

"The person without a purpose is like a ship without a rudder."

—Thomas Carlyle

Before we worry too much about what our purpose *is,* let's talk about the purpose of our purpose. One of the curses of having consciousness is all the damn questions we ask ourselves. Namely, what's it all about? Why are we here?

If you're reading this book it's safe to say you've been wrestling with your own existence and higher purpose for a while. Don't worry, you're not alone. Philosophers and scholars have been trying to define our existence for millennia.

The ironic piece of the puzzle is that our existence and our purpose can't be defined for a species, it has to be defined for an individual. We can't be told what our purpose is, we have to define it for ourselves. Humanity is such a pain in the ass.

For us to remain sane and not continuously dread our own mortality, we must find a reason for our existence. We must have a reason to exist. That reason is not defined by our love for puppies or crocheting, it's defined in how we honor our values and serve the greater good.

Trying to define your purpose by writing down your current interests or reviewing your browsing history is not going to give you insight into your soul, it's only going to show you all the distractions and emotional pacifiers you use to soothe yourself from the fact that you're not living in alignment with your greater purpose.

An important concept you need to accept as you continue reading and seeking your authentic self is that, like happiness, your Identity & Purpose do not need to be discovered, they need to be allowed.

Your authentic self, your identity, and your purpose already exist inside you. Unfortunately, you inherited some rules and beliefs early in life that caused you to suppress or even ignore what makes you unique.

It's those unchecked beliefs and, believe it or not, our inherent talents that can divert us from our true purpose. I have held a lot of roles in my life not because they were aligned with my core beliefs and values, but because I was good at them.

> *Barbie has worked in I.T. for the better part of her adult life. She is organized, detail focused, and disciplined. She does quality work at a pace and output that is acceptable to her management. She enjoys a standard raise every year and, even with the amount of turnover in her industry, is confident she'll always have a "good job" which makes her family very happy. And she's miserable.*

Because of the compartmentalization of her industry, Barbie rarely sees or communicates with other members of her team. Almost all correspondence is done virtually or electronically. Additionally, she only sees a sliver of the overall work and because of her experience often repeats the same work over and over.

Her top Zone Moment includes getting removed from a large project because she spoke up in a group meeting against the project manager who completely ignored her recommendations and nearly ruined six months worth of work by blindly accepting new terms from the client.

But she also recalled the time when she was "volunteered" for the role of PTA chairperson and during her tenure, she was able to significantly increase the amount of funds raised by tossing out the old fundraising activities and introducing new initiatives that she knew would better align with the community's interests and (yup) values.

Both of these events allowed Barbie to reflect on and accept where her strengths and interests lay. That's not to say that she didn't enjoy I.T. and particularly loved fundraising, but it did give her the ammunition she needed to realize that the environment *was just as important as the task.*

She accepted that she valued cooperation and needed to contribute to the larger initiative at a level that her day job couldn't provide, so by remaining on the PTA she was able to satisfy those needs and find a new level of acceptance and satisfaction in her career as well as make connections and contribute to her community in a significant way.

This is again where I think the pursuit of passions confuses and lets us down. Just because I'm a talented martial artist doesn't mean that my purpose is to practice or teach martial arts for the rest of my life.

It's fun, it makes me happy, it honors my values of fitness and adventure, but its practice does not give my life meaning. In fact, too much of it actually distracts me from my higher purpose. I understand, too, that the tools and medium of a purpose are not in themselves a purpose. My purpose is not to be an author, my purpose is to help everyone discover their value. I'm currently realizing my purpose *through* authoring this book.

I may use books, podcasts, e-courses, and coaching to accomplish that, but they're just the tools I use to express my true purpose. Learning to differentiate between the value of passions and the meaning of purpose will go a long way towards helping you feel accomplished, valued, and confident.

I'll present later in the book some of the most common ways we sabotage ourselves and prevent ourselves from living our authentic purpose, conquering many of which have their own categories in the self-help genre.

It has been my experience (and the experience of a couple hundred of my clients) that the solution to our self-esteem, confidence, codependency, you-name-it issues isn't a tactic to address them individually but to address the root cause. More often than not, the root cause of our angst is not knowing who we are or why we matter.

It's safe to say I (and probably you) have taken every available personality, leadership, communication, relationship, and vocational aptitude test available in the pursuit of my true identity. And they all provided the same result: Congratulations! You can be whatever you want to be! Blech.

I have spent far too many hours fantasizing about discovering some long-dormant skill or talent that would lay out the roadmap of my life. That I would be at a party and pick up a random instrument and know instinctively how to play it. That I have the soul of a cursed wizard in me and on my 18th birthday (long passed) I would awaken and be imbued with magical powers. Fate sealed. Purpose discovered.

Alas, what I have come to discover is that purpose is not found in skill or talent (both of which can be learned and/or developed with hard work), but instead purpose is the expression of the best, authentic versions of ourselves.

Your purpose isn't a hobby, your purpose isn't a fad. Your purpose is timeless and limitless. Your purpose defines you as much as you define it. Your purpose keeps you up one night and lets you sleep soundly the next. Your purpose surrounds you and supports you. Yup, it's the Force!

Your purpose cannot be discovered on a vision board or through countless affirmations (don't even get me started). Your purpose cannot be manifested or revealed to you. You and your purpose are one and the same. Your purpose isn't something you pursue, it's something that consumes you. Your purpose isn't a person, place, or thing. Your purpose is its action.

So what is our purpose then?

So far our discussion about Identity & Purpose has been focused on learning about those nonnegotiable parts of us that must be honored and expressed. We've accepted that our identity isn't something that must be discovered, but uncovered and allowed to flourish. That identity is essential for us to define our true purpose in life.

Please let me be very clear (I have some baggage) I'm talking about *purpose*, not *passion*. Passion is a fool's errand, passion is play, passion is an indulgence. Passion is external. I'm talking about the kind of purpose that changes the world. Our world. Their world. The world.

Evidence of your purpose is scattered throughout your life. Regardless of any of your circumstances or the impression you have of yourself, I am confident there have been multiple occasions in your life that have inspired and fulfilled you like no others.

Moments, exchanges, and events in our lives that illicit a visceral physical and emotional response within us are indications that (as we've discussed) our values and needs are in full play. Whether through challenge or serendipity, we were completely focused on and invested at the moment.

These Zone Moments let us know that the circumstances surrounding them are very closely aligned to our core purpose and beliefs, either by honoring or violating them.

EXERCISE 8

Write the essay of your own Zone Moment.

Imagine a scenario either imaginary or recalled from a movie or book in which you are the star character. What is the challenge that must be overcome? What skills make you the perfect person to overcome that challenge?

Who is your supporting cast? What are their skills? How do their attributes complement yours? How do they contribute to the cause?

What is the outcome? How are you rewarded? What gives you the greatest sense of accomplishment or satisfaction?

Revisit this story frequently during your journey. Revise it as you reject old beliefs and assert new ones.

That essay of your ideal Zone Moment has powerful insight into your purpose.

In his segment during Leadercast 2015, Pastor Andy Stanley asked a very powerful question of the audience. His presentation topic was leadership and bravery and inevitably he addressed the nagging question we all face about doing great work. What should we do?

Some would say we should focus on our strengths, others would say to do thorough market research, still others would say to find your bliss. The dogma we've all been presented is that the secret to a happy and meaningful life is to "do what you love." But Andy and I actually share a different perspective on discovering your greater purpose.

When I look at the great and infamous accomplishments of the world I don't see people gleefully pursuing their joy or their hobby. I see people who saw something that *broke their heart* so completely that they could not stand by and watch for one moment longer. So they took action.

Your purpose is the thing that will get you out of bed at 3 AM when you just managed to crawl in at 2 AM. Your purpose is what will not allow you to take "No" or "Can't" or "Impossible" as answers. Your purpose is the thing that you don't seek permission or approval to pursue.

Your purpose is a wellspring of energy and focus because it stems from the molten core of your being. Your purpose you would do for free, alone, uphill, in the snow, twice because you cannot tolerate it not being done.

When Pastor Andy asked that question of me, "What breaks your heart?" I knew immediately what breaks my heart, what had always broken my heart and it was watching people suffer who did not know their own value.

If you are lost, adrift, confused, aimless and believe all the things people (including yourself) have told you are wrong with you...you are breaking my heart and I will not stand for it.

Today, if you ask me my purpose I will simply say, "Everyone has value." It's a statement, a mantra, and a guidepost to everything I do. It may not make a lot of sense to you, but it doesn't need to make sense to you, it's *my* purpose. When I have to decide to do or not do something I use my purpose to guide my decision. Will this help someone discover their true value?

Your purpose is equally as fundamental to your being. I can't restate Pastor Andy's question any more eloquently. If you're looking for purpose, start with what breaks your heart, what you would go to war over, what you want to bring to or eradicate from the world, and set about doing it.

That, my friend, is your purpose.

SECTION II

Action!

CHAPTER 5

Decision-Making

*"You cannot make progress without
making decisions."*

— Jim Rohn

Congratulations!

Believe it or not, by completing Section 1 you've taken a signif-icant step towards clarifying your authentic identity and designing a life of purpose. I know, I know, you want to know "now what?" and we're getting to that. The intent of Section 1's Assessment Phase was to help us understand ourselves, our motives, and our criteria for success. Section 2's Action Phase is where we start to have some fun and put the information we've gathered to good use.

Decision-making is where the rubber meets the road in our lives. Decision-making is where we either honor or violate our values on a continual basis. Decision-making is how we move closer to or further from the existence of our dreams. If you're looking around your life right now and you're not happy with what you see, odds are you used some faulty decision-making to get here.

And if you don't know what choices to make at all, Section 1 is the framework for choosing your path forward. If knowing is half the battle, choosing is the other half.

Consider the classic midlife crisis. It's not much unlike an annual performance appraisal at work, except it's an internal comparison of what we thought we wanted, who we thought we were, and what we're actually doing. When people have these types of identity crises they often ask, "How did I get here?"

Poor, or more accurately, absent-minded decision-making, that's how.

That's not to say that you purposely or carelessly made bad choices (I mean, spring break is spring break), but more likely you made your decisions on poor criteria or for the wrong reasons. As we discussed in Section 1, we're making hundreds, thousands of decisions each and every day, and those choices are being influenced by our instincts of survival, belonging, and status. And cumulatively, they create our reality.

Those survival instincts rarely ever align with our long-term goals for happiness or purpose. Not only that, but those motives are also almost always inherited from our parents, friends, society, and false identity and often don't actually represent what we truly believe about ourselves or the life we want. When we self-sabotage or avoid challenge or conflict it's because we are choosing what's expected or safe, not necessarily what's best for our souls.

When I discovered how many choices I was making that were an attempt to receive approval and limit myself to align with other peoples' definitions of me I was shocked. My career, my body, my finances, my attitude, and my very personality were being limited by my choices. And those choices were in turn being made unconsciously.

Once I became a father something inside me switched. Becoming a parent is a significant moment for most of us and I was both elated and terrified. Without much to go on, my brain scrambled for direction and instruction and, sneaky little sucker that it is, it found a bunch of instructions buried in my subconscious.

There were hundreds of comments and expectations that I had accepted without question when I was a child about what it meant to be a "good" father. A good father did this, not that. A good father said this, not that. A good father shows this, not that. Without much thought or consideration, I had all the parenting gaps plugged. But at what cost?

I don't fault the sources; as people who genuinely cared about me, I understand that they wanted me to be safe, not necessarily happy. Remember that. That's what tribes do, we keep each other safe, we don't necessarily make each other happy.

> **PRO TIP: The people who love and care about you the most don't want you to be happy (even when they say they do), they want you to be safe.**

So, not too long into fatherhood, I found myself acting out of character. Making choices, not based on my values and needs, but according to the expectations and beliefs of others, and I was not happy with what I saw in myself. That's how it happens.

That's how we create a reality that is in conflict with our authentic selves. Well, one of the ways.

Charlie (yup, me) had been unemployed for eight months when he got the call to join the national laboratory in New Mexico. In addition to (finally) getting an offer of employment, the role was a perfect fit for his experience, career goals, and the compensation package was terrific.

He and his wife were already estranged, having been sleeping in separate rooms for about a year, so in some ways it felt like an opportunity to pull the trigger on their looming divorce. And he'd always wanted to move "out west."

The bills had been piling up and the credit union was talking about foreclosure. Though it may not sound like much of a decision, Charlie paused. He didn't want to pull his kids from the town where they had lived for the past several (very formative) years, but he wondered about how he could possibly be a good father from 1847 miles away?

Good fathers, he had been told, come home every night, they help with homework, they keep their kids safe, and are a part of their children's lives day in and day out. A good father wouldn't move 1847 miles away and leave them.

He worried about what people would think, especially his kids and even their mother. He wrestled with this decision for a while, but then he did something very powerful and decided not to make the decision based on anyone else's expectations about fatherhood other than his own. He wrote down everything he had been taught about being a good father and then he asked himself if he really believed those things.

Finally, he wrote down what mattered most to him about being a good father. Things like teaching his kids to embrace their strengths, to learn their own values, to question everything (even what he had taught them), and to create the best opportunities possible for them, wherever it took him.

Though he would be physically removed from their lives, he realized that this sacrifice was more valuable than the alternatives of staying in a toxic and dysfunctional marriage possibly teaching them harmful lessons about how relationships are supposed to work, accepting a marginal role with little hope for advancement or financial prosperity, or potentially resenting his role as their father because of some presumed "sacrifice."

When Charlie finally accepted the position and packed his truck for the drive, he did it with the peace of mind that he was doing it in alignment with his values and even honoring his own needs. In doing so he also became a better father by demonstrating all those things he had been trying to teach his kids about fulfilling their own needs and dreams.

Charlie and his kids are closer than ever thanks to FaceTime and frequent flyer miles.

To create a fulfilling and happy life that meets each of our needs we need to learn to make decisions on criteria that are always aligned with our best interests. Those criteria were covered in Section 1: our values and emotional needs.

In his bestselling book and through his center in Atlanta, Georgia, Dr. Aubrey C. Daniels defines a behavioral model that hinges on our interpretation of consequences. He presents the ABC model as a way for us to understand what triggers us to make choices and then what influences the choices we make.

The ABC model defines every choice being initiated by a trigger event or antecedent (A), that elicits a behavior (B), which yields a certain consequence (C). The likelihood of us repeating a certain behavior is dependent on how we perceive the consequence. That is to say, we do what we do because of what happens to us when we do it.

But, not all consequences are created equal. Also from Dr. Daniels' model is the concept that some consequences are more powerful than others. He argues, quite convincingly, that positive consequences (reinforcement) have an astonishing power to elicit change in our lives.

To apply this power in our own lives we need to break down consequences into their constituent parts: reinforcement, timing, and reliability.

Reinforcement is either positive (P) or negative (N). Timing is either immediate (I) or future (F). And reliability is either certain (C) or uncertain (U). When we evaluate consequences in our lives and their power to influence us, timing and reliability have a significant impact on our association of cause and effect. Immediate-Certain (*IC) results imprint on us heavily.

So what does this have to do with our ability to discover our Identity & Purpose? Well, when it comes to our decision-making, it's important for us to consider how we're reinforcing ourselves. Understanding these influences also helps us understand why we keep doing what we're doing even if it isn't getting us the results we want.

> *Consider two drivers approaching a traffic light as it turns yellow the first day they receive their driver's licenses. The first driver stomps on the gas and sails through the intersection unscathed, making it to their destination on time and uninterrupted (positive reinforcement). The second driver stomps on the gas and, in their haste, crashes into another car (negative reinforcement). Because of their individual experiences, it's easy to predict their behaviors when they encounter another yellow light. Driver 1 is likely to repeat their past successful behavior and run the light. Driver 2 is likely to hit the brakes.*

These types of calculations and evidence-weighing are going on in our minds constantly, but it's even more insidious than that because we will use past, unrelated consequences to influence future, similar situations and decisions. Or worse, we'll apply someone else's beliefs about us, our capabilities, or what's best for us in our decision-making.

When we engage in this absenteeism decision-making we're creating a life that is nowhere near the life we would choose for ourselves. Also, if we make choices based on our mood, company, or energy level we make those decisions based on short-term influences and outcomes and not necessarily on our true purpose or goals. This book hopes to remedy that outcome.

If we instead make decisions based on an unwavering set of criteria and priorities, we can slowly but surely nudge our life in a direction that is more aligned with our authentic selves and greater purpose. This sounds like a lot of work, doesn't it? Exhausting, complicated. Ugh.

Well, what if I told you that making decisions based on fulfilling our own emotional needs in alignment with our values was actually positively reinforcing and *easier* than the constant weighing, guessing, and doubt of making choices by other peoples' criteria? It's true.

I'm not going to recreate all of Dr. Daniels' work here, so I'll skip to the important bit: positive reinforcement wins every single time, hands down. Positive reinforcement is more sustainable, more powerful, more influential, and more efficient than negative reinforcement every day of the week.

That's not to say that negative reinforcement doesn't have its place. Yelling "No!" when someone is about to grab a hot pan or slapping away an unwanted advance are effective, even necessary, when an immediate, short-term correction is required. But at some point negative reinforcements lose their effectiveness and other measures are required.

When you make choices that conflict with your core beliefs and values you are in fact violating yourself and creating negative reinforcement. Not only do you not get what's best for you, but you also create an environment where you feel shame and disappointment in yourself for having done so.

You instinctively know better, but you do it anyway. We all do. Until we don't.

We typically encounter a couple of obstacles as we work to change our decision-making habits and we'll discuss them in greater detail in Section 3, but right now we need to address the #1 influence for resisting this strategy...belief.

Making significant changes in your life requires you to believe that you have the power to do so. Accepting that you have the ability to manipulate your surroundings through *choice*, and that choice is what determines your outcomes, are paramount to your success. And finally, you need to realize that your choices must be aligned to honoring your values and fulfilling your needs to be beneficial.

Now listen, as I have pointed out, I'm not an idiot. I realize we live in a society, with responsibilities, and that we can't always just do what we want to do. Ironically, there are consequences. But, there are far more opportunities to choose alignment to our values than not. Choosing whether to scroll aimlessly through social media or read this book was a choice, and clearly you made a brilliant one.

The final point I want to make about decisions is the concept of multiple choice versus essay answers. For many of us, life is a constant stream of multiple choice or true-false challenges. We blindly accept that we must accept from a prepopulated set of outcomes or answers. Chicken or fish. Beach or mountains. Coke or Pepsi.

Ironically, we live in a time with more choices than ever before in every aspect of our lives, from where we live, to what careers we pursue, to our lifestyle choices. But even given the number of choices, we still feel like we have little power or control over those choices.

The reason for this is because of the immense pressure we feel from those well-meaning sources we've already called out: parents, family, friends, etc. The way to combat this and ensure you're choosing the outcome that best aligns with your authentic life is to derive your own answer before even considering the options offered to you.

As a member of the U.S. Navy and commercial nuclear power communities, I can promise you I've taken more exams than I could possibly count. Many of them were multiple choice. And if you've taken a few in your past you know that multiple-choice exams are written specifically to trick us by providing one correct answer, one obviously wrong answer, and two half-correct answers.

As a way to deal with those very cleverly written half-correct answers, I was taught a technique that I recommend to all my clients. *Before you ever read any of the answers presented, write your own answer.*

Read the question, then write your own essay answer. Once you've done that you can choose the option that most closely aligns with the answer you thought was correct before getting tricked by the half-correct answers.

In life, this means defining your outcome beforehand. Before you start swiping through the options presented to you by a dating app, do you even know what you absolutely *must* have in a potential partner? What about what your perfect match must *not* do or be?

Instead of limiting your decisions to the options presented to you (by people or systems with different criteria and motives than you) write down and understand *your* correct answer, then go about making that choice your only option. An authentic life requires essay answers.

EXERCISE 9

Think of an upcoming choice or decision you have to make, maybe it's a job search or maybe you're thinking of tossing your hat back into the dating pool.

Before you open an app or submit a Google search use your values and needs profile to determine the critical characteristics necessary for that choice to align to your values and fulfill your needs.

Don't let your expectations of available options influence your ideal outcome, but be realistic ($1B salary for a

1hr/wk job is wasting your time). Writing out the perfect option or solution as it pertains to your values and needs is the goal of this exercise.

Once you've completed your description of your ideal outcome, then you've actually made a choice. Now you can proceed with your search and be confident you are making informed and intelligent compromises or consolations based on the available options.

Mastering your decision-making is the most powerful skill you can learn in order to change your circumstances and create the life of your dreams. Accepting that the only things you can actually control are your state and your choices is paramount to living in alignment with your Identity & Purpose. Next, we're going to use these skills to start creating activities and practices that nourish us and make us the master of fulfilling our own needs through self-care.

CHAPTER 6

Self-Care

"Knowing how to be solitary is central to the art of loving. When we can be alone, we can be with others without using them as a means of escape."

— bell hooks

When I ask new clients, "Tell me about your self-care routine," they inevitably tell me about getting a massage (when everybody else has plans) or reading a book (when everybody else has plans), or soaking in a bathtub (when everybody else has plans).

But like all other influences in our lives, engaging in proper self-care isn't about doing what's popular or prescribed externally, it's about one thing and one thing only: the outcome. The purpose of self-care is to maintain proper physical, emotional, and mental health so that we're firing on all cylinders.

Show me someone who's performing at their best every day, moving closer to their life's greater purpose, and making a positive impact on the world and I'll show you someone with a healthy self-care routine.

A healthy self-care schedule is important because it helps maintain one's overall health. It can aid in avoiding burnout, depression, anxiety, and other mental health issues. Self-care is also important because it helps with emotional stability. It keeps people from being overwhelmed by their emotions or unable to control negative thoughts and reactions.

Executed properly it also boosts motivation and mood through physical care which is needed for productivity. Most people's idea of self-care is taking a day, or worse, a couple of hours, to recover because they're completely burned-out, stressed, and feeling like they're about to crack.

That type of self-care is "corrective," but proper self-care is executed "preventively," meaning it's the little, medium, and large things we do for ourselves every day, month, or year to maintain optimum mental, physical, and emotional health.

In order to move forward together, you must reframe your idea of what self-care is, what it is not, and what its purpose is in our lives. Don't worry, I'm going to help you. The reason I know you'll experience objections and resistance to my instructions is because if you were a bit more selfish or didn't put everyone else's needs ahead of your own, you wouldn't be struggling with defining your Identity & Purpose.

PRO TIP: Self-care is about ensuring you're the best possible version of yourself at all times, ironically so that you can do as much as possible for others through your life's purpose.

HOW TO TAKE CARE OF YOURSELF PHYSICALLY

It is important to remember that your physical health is just as important as your mental health. Your physical ability will play a huge role in the quality of your life.

One of the best things you can do for your physical self is to maintain a healthy, nourishing diet free from excessive sugar, caffeine, and alcohol. Eating well will help you feel more energized and ready to work out or go about your day. Make sure you're getting enough protein, carbohydrates, and fats. It may take some time to figure out what foods make up a healthy diet for you, but it's worth it!

Exercise is important too. It doesn't have to be complicated—even something like going on a short walk can make a difference. The key thing about exercising is that you should do it every day—don't wait until the weekend when you're overwhelmed with your to-do list.

What's the "best" exercise program for you? The one you'll actually do!

Don't adopt the latest fitness trend because it's been scientif-ically proven or takes half the time and none of the effort. That's classic marketing speak to convince you that your current plan is not good enough or behind the times and you'll end up chasing your tail without much to show for it. Use your values and needs to define what "fit" means to you and then choose a program specifically designed to achieve those results.

Remember that every choice you make in life should align with your values and needs, so make choices that motivate and positively reinforce you. The key to achieving that is to reflect back on your routine and how you used to play as a child. The secret to long-term fitness is play! If fitness is fun and you consider it a reward, you will actually look forward to it and make time to do it.

HOW TO TAKE CARE OF YOURSELF SOCIALLY

When we think about care, we usually think about taking care of other people. Social care is a powerful way to build resilience and find meaning in life. It's a way to give back and a way to receive. Even if you consider yourself an introvert, you still need to feel like a member of a group no matter how infrequently. This section will help you identify ways in which you can take care of yourself socially.

Social care is the act of connecting with your community. It's about finding meaning in life and having an opportunity to give. There are many ways that individuals can practice social care, such as volunteering, donating resources, or participating in simple acts of kindness like holding open a door for someone or buying someone a coffee.

In the workplace, it is important that managers have an understanding of how social care influences organizational culture so they can create an environment where employees feel valued and cared for at work. If you're one of those leaders, don't wait any longer to take steps to ensure a positive work environment.

All this, though, needs to be weighed against your emotional needs profile. For those of us who don't rank love & connection or contribution very highly, the necessity to perform acts of service may not be a powerful driver and can also be demotivating and draining. Again, don't force yourself to do what other people (myself included) tell you is "right."

HOW TO TAKE CARE OF YOURSELF MENTALLY

No discussion of health would be complete without discussing what healthy sleep looks like. Despite what you might hear you cannot function on three hours of sleep each night for long.

A lot of people think that they can function on a little sleep, or no sleep at all. The current "hustle" culture has imposed some pretty ridiculous and unsustainable standards for success. But the reality is that it might be better for your mental health to give up some hustle time for sleep. If you don't take care of yourself mentally, then you won't be able to take care of yourself physically or emotionally either.

Starting each day with a quarter tank of fuel means you're not going to make it to your final destination. The most common causes for poor sleep include stress, improper exercise too close to bedtime, too much snacking close to bedtime, alcohol or caffeine, sharing your bed with children or pets, light and noise pollution, poor routines (or lack thereof), and overall physical discomfort. Being intentional about your sleep environment is essential to getting the most out of the hours you have to sleep.

Also, if everybody in the house has a new mattress, set bedtime, and evening wind-down routine except you, it's safe to say that you're not taking care of yourself. It is important to maintain a healthy mental state of mind if you want to stay productive and happy throughout the day.

Well, it's important to maintain a regular schedule for sleeping and waking up. That way, your internal clock will be synchronized with your natural circadian rhythms. It's also recommendable to take time for yourself every day, through meditation or mindfulness exercises. This will provide you with an opportunity to disconnect from work and just focus on your mind and body.

CREATING SELF-CARE ACTIVITIES

Self-care is about maintaining your emotional, physical, and intellectual energy levels at their peaks through activities that you design and control for yourself. By learning to fulfill your own needs in a healthy way, you can free yourself from approval and permission-seeking behaviors and make choices that are in your best interests.

Great self-care activities, by my definition, can be found at the intersection of your values and your emotional needs. If our values are "what" is important to us, and emotional needs are "how" we need to experience the world, self-care is the way we honor our values in a manner that fulfills our emotional needs.

Take one of my self-care activities, for example, my Sunday hikes.

Being in nature has a multitude of benefits, namely the rejuvenation of our feminine energy (hence: Mother Nature), but for me, it's a way to honor my value of adventure! Any creature I encounter, a bird, a lizard, a chipmunk—even just their tracks—makes me feel like a kid again. No matter how seemingly insignificant, encountering animals or tracks fills me with a sense of wonder, appreciation, and yup, adventure. So, among other benefits, my hikes are a way to honor my values.

But, that doesn't quite make it the super soul charging self-care I was hoping for. There's another component, another dimension that needs to be acknowledged to make a regular old hike fulfill me and that's addressing my emotional needs.

My #1 top emotional need is contribution. No question. Always has been, most likely always will be. So, in order to turbocharge my value of adventure and qualify my hikes as self-care, I need to feel a sense of contribution as well.

So, how could I add a level of contribution to a hike in nature?

My solution is to volunteer with my local trail maintenance group. So now when I hike I can perform a service simultaneously. I'm honoring my need for adventure while contributing to my community. Win-Win.

OK, so what?

So in order to properly design and execute solid, sustainable, enriching self-care, you need to put aside the notion that self-care just means pampering yourself when time and opportunity allow.

And men, you need to let go of the stigma that self-care is only about embracing your feminine side.

EXERCISE 10

Select one of your values, either one that is most important to you or one that you identified as being underserved and create a scheduled activity that you can participate in to honor that value.

Start small, cheap, and quick. It doesn't have to be an around-the-world cruise. In fact, small, seemingly effortless forms of self-care are a way for us to gently accept that our needs are important and worthy of attention.

Finally, think of a way to honor that value through your top emotional need. If it's love & connection maybe you can enjoy this activity with others; if it's uncertainty maybe there's a way to randomize the activity like volunteering at a charity where your duties will vary from visit to visit.

The true power of self-care is that it acts as rocket fuel for your goals and self-esteem. An added benefit of getting serious about your self-care is the message you are sending to your subconscious about your priorities and boundaries.

When you suppress your needs and violate your own values you're basically telling yourself that you're not that important. This begets self-sabotage and self-limiting beliefs. "I know I said I wanted to take that class on Wednesday nights, but somebody's really got to fold this laundry."

DIVERSE SELF-CARE

The truth is that a bulletproof self-care routine consists of a diverse set of activities. We're going to bust some myths about self-care and the first is that self-care requires a whole day, or weekend, to be effective. Some are simple, quick, free; others are more complex, take more time, and require an investment.

Obviously, the smaller the investment, the smaller the return, but even tiny acts of kindness (to yourself) have meaning and can improve your overall outlook.

Also, if you have only one self-care activity, you're likely ignoring the majority of your emotional needs. If my Sunday hikes were the only way I recharged or tried to fulfill *all* my emotional needs I think you can see how underserved I would be.

What about my need for growth & knowledge? Love & connection?

Ensuring we have designed a life that addresses each of our needs, no matter how insignificant we may think they are, ensures we are stable and secure and don't engage in any mindless habits or behavior that are subconsciously an attempt to meet our needs.

Having each of our needs' buckets filled by our own action keeps us grounded and centered, and allows for better decision-making and mindfulness. Knowing that we control the flow of the fulfillment of our needs reduces anxiety and neediness.

So, much like the exercise we engaged in to assess our values' honors and violations, we will now take steps to assess our self-care regime. Think about your self-care in different time scales: daily, weekly, monthly, annually. Think about your self-care across your different needs: contribution, certainty, significance, etc.

Go easy on yourself. Start small and don't make your self-care a burden or a "to-do" that could quickly create shame and disappointment if you miss the mark. Self-care should never be a task to complete or a measuring stick of your self-worth. These are things you do for yourself.

The objective of self-care is always to serve your emotional needs through your values.

INTENTIONAL

Intentionality around the care of yourself means you're not waiting until your emotional battery is at 1% to take action. It means you connect yourself to your emotional charger each day for a quick charge, each week for a full charge, and occasionally for a self-indulgent over-charge.

Self-care is an important part of every person's life. A lot of people don't prioritize it because they are either too busy or feel guilty for taking time for themselves. Scheduling your self-care also makes you a priority in your life and creates healthy bound-aries (which we'll discuss in more detail pretty soon).

Finally, regular self-care will help you shed old beliefs about who you are and adopt the habits of your true identity. We are the sum total of all our experiences, so if you've ever had a bad experience with someone or something, you might have some lingering resentment towards that person or thing.

This is called an "energetic attachment"—it's just a side effect of being human. But when these attachments are allowed to linger on the energetic level, they can create obstacles that will prevent you from living up to your highest potential. Repeating or ruminating about those attachments are a contributor to your repeating unhealthy, self-defeating behaviors. Healthy self-care activities replace those old habits with new, healthy ones.

CHAPTER 7

Boundaries

"The only real conflict you will ever have in your life won't be with others, but with yourself."

— Shannon L. Alder

So now that we know who we are and what's important to us, what do we do about it? How do we protect and enforce these expectations and standards for living that we've defined? (Hint: it's in the chapter title.)

When I shared that I was including a chapter in this book about boundaries, a friend wrote, "It better be good because there's already a book about that out there!" The truth is there are already *lots* of books out there about most of the topics that I'm sharing with you. The difference is that what I'm sharing with you is actionable and uncovers a lot of what "they" got wrong or glossed over.

As I am going to show you, boundaries, as they relate to Identity & Purpose, are not about imposing our will or beliefs on other people. Typical dogma around boundaries dictates how other people should treat you. Wrong. They say that boundaries are about saying "no." Wrong. They say that boundaries are about achieving your priorities and goals. Wrong.

In fact, much of what we believe about boundaries carries a negative connotation, which is why many of us are bad at setting and reinforcing them or don't have any at all. Boundaries are typically considered to be confrontational and imposing, but that, too, is wrong.

Earlier I described that I assess my happiness by comparing the number of instances my values are honored against the times they are violated. If my values are honored more than they are violated, I'm generally happy (as you would be too).

The true purpose and benefit of having healthy boundaries is to protect your values and therefore your identity. And that responsibility is yours and yours alone. Boundaries are not set to control others, they're set to alert you to pending values violations and, by association, to protect your happiness.

If you want to think of boundaries as a fence, fine, but consider that this fence isn't set up to keep other people out, it's set to keep your way of life in. At the end of the day we can't really control other people anyway, so why not focus our effort where it really matters: on controlling our own behavior.

Boundaries are:	Boundaries aren't:
• Proactive	• Reactive
• Intentional	• Reflexive
• Positive	• Controlling
• Healthy	• Dictation
• Values-based	• Emotionally-based

The first shift you need to make when you set new boundaries is to focus on setting the boundary around your own behavior. Think of a healthy boundary as an alarm that you're approaching a hazard. In this case, the hazard is a violation of a value.

As an example, I value fitness. As such, my self-care routine around this value dictates that I'll exercise at least five times per week. My workout time is on my calendar so clients can't book over it and so that I don't rely on my mood or energy level to decide whether or not I'm going to have time to exercise. I've set a boundary (in combination with my self-care routine) that I will exercise *at least* five times per week.

If by day six of the week I've only exercised four times...I'm in danger of violating that value. Within reason, I am not going to violate that value and I protect it by honoring my boundary and taking steps to meet my goal of exercising five times per week.

OK, that was a pretty easy example, I know. But it was supposed to be. When it comes to boundaries though, we do have responsibilities related to their establishment and enforcement.

Debbie recognized pretty quickly that she modified her behavior around men that she was romantically interested in. She was overly accommodating and constantly sought their attention and approval. All of this added up to her quickly deprioritizing her plans whenever they called.

Dating was definitely a priority to her, but Debbie realized that she was spending a lot of time and effort on relationships that weren't necessarily reciprocal or were at a minimum detracting from her attention to available men.

Basically, she was participating in half-dates, where she was investing a lot of her hopes and dreams of a romantic relationship in men who didn't necessarily feel the same about her. But some of these men were good friends with whom she shared some common interests and activities, so it was getting messy.

So, after a careful review of her needs and values Debbie set a healthy, values-based boundary around her social interactions. She decided she would no longer spend one-on-one time with men that she felt romantically interested in unless they clearly felt the same attraction.

When any of those men would ask to do something together, Debbie would ask if it was just going to be the two of them or if the larger group was invited as well. Whenever a romantic interest invited her to do something alone she would simply state her boundary.

It might seem awkward and uncomfortable for you to read, but it made it very clear to the men in her life that her private time was precious and devoted to the pursuit of her romantic interests. And if the men in her life were not interested in her romantically, she'd see them at softball practice or the next group gathering.

DECLARE

Firstly, it has been my experience that external violations of my boundaries are almost always unintentional. In the most loving way possible I have to tell you that nobody's thinking about you. They're not. They're thinking about what you're thinking about: themselves.

So, the first responsibility we have related to our boundaries is to declare them. Now, that doesn't mean you need a PowerPoint to inform everyone in your life about your boundaries—yuck. Not even your MeeMaw would sit through that. But, you do owe the people in your life (even established ones) the benefit of the doubt that they are completely unaware of your boundaries.

So, in a healthy, values-led way it's your job to inform people of when they are infringing on a boundary. Have you ever heard the expression "Swears like a sailor"? Well, I *am* a sailor. So sometimes my conversational language violates some peoples' boundaries around the use of colorful metaphors and colloquialisms.

This book lost almost 2000 words when I removed all the colorful language.

The point is, anytime someone is confident enough to inform me that I'm infringing on their boundary I have an opportunity to accommodate. We are both now fully aware of the boundary. This applies equally to the act of defining and declaring boundaries to yourself.

In general, we can usually brush off external values violations and boundary infringements pretty easily, but when we violate them ourselves, we risk a downward spiral of shame and low self-esteem. Now that you have defined your values, you have no excuse for unintentionally violating them.

PROTECT

Step two is about protecting and enforcing the boundary. Once declared, both parties now have a choice to honor or ignore the now-defined boundary. Does anyone have the right to tell me what language I can use? Not really. I mean, I know there are social conventions and expectations, but I still have a choice. But that choice has consequences.

The key to being taken seriously and having your boundaries respected lies in your consistency and sincerity around them. Again, if you have established them as prescribed, with the intent of protecting your values, it's going to be hard for anyone to argue that they're unjust or unreasonable. Additionally, if they are values-based you will be more likely to be consistent and confident about their establishment and reinforcement, even with yourself.

The most important takeaway to protecting your boundaries, though, is what it does for your self-esteem and self-worth. Most of our identity challenges hinge on the message we received, one way or another, that our needs were not important, or that our values and opinions did not matter.

Because of that message, and more importantly, because we believed that message, we have systematically violated and/or repressed our values and needs. The expression of that belief about ourselves is that we are not comfortable demonstrating or enforcing our needs, values, or boundaries.

Protecting our boundaries may feel uncomfortable at first, but if we can define healthy values-based boundaries and hold ourselves accountable to them, we can eventually and gradually gain confidence in that identity and feel comfortable asserting them externally.

This brings us back to the concept of the consequences for our choices and boundary violations.

REACT

At some point, we will have to deal with repeated boundary violations. Either internally or externally, we live in a society where the world cannot possibly revolve around each and every one of us all of the time. This is where and how values-based boundaries are so powerful.

I cannot overstate how important it is to your health and happiness to consistently honor your values and limit the number of violations you accept to a minimum. Knowingly allowing your boundaries to be continually violated is a recipe for misery, frustration, and self-pity.

Maybe you're experiencing this right now in your life by working for a boss or in an industry that violates your value system. Or remaining in a relationship that does the same. Neither of those scenarios is sustainable.

Eventually, we must make a choice. Eventually, we must decide whether or not our values, and by extension our identity, is worth defending and protecting. Repeated violations of boundaries must be addressed either through action or inaction. Either by choosing to engage or disengage with the violator, even if it's yourself.

Every situation is different and there is no one perfect course of action for every person in every scenario, but trust me when I say that you will never be truly happy or fulfilled, and therefore never reach your full potential, until you are willing to respect and defend your boundaries.

CONSEQUENCES

So why would we willingly allow our boundaries to be violated over and over again? There is an argument that people with low self-esteem and low self-worth may have a greater susceptibility to violations of boundaries.

This is because they are looking for acceptance from the world and will do anything to get it. It's also because they might not have the tools or knowledge on how to maintain healthy boundaries. When we consider that at some point we will have to deal with repeated boundary violations, one of the most important things is having a sense of self-worth and self-esteem.

Approval seeking and attachment to outcome are the two main forces working to deprive us of our identity and self-worth. If we fear the loss or disapproval of others we will willingly allow ourselves to be pushed around and walked over rather than assert our boundaries.

Unfortunately, this typically results in a catch-22 where we lack self-esteem allowing boundary violations, and the boundary violations lead to low self-esteem. The answer to both is having a strong sense of self through clearly defined values and needs. (I know, I'm a broken record.)

This is especially challenging when the boundary violator is someone whom we love and care for. Their approval and acceptance is so important to us that we are willing, and sometimes feel obligated, to accept their betrayal. This too is a dead end.

Never is it more frustrating than to have boundaries continually ignored by family members. The very people who are supposed to love and accept us the most are often the primary sources of our limiting beliefs and boundary testing. Like bulls in a china shop.

In part, their behavior and seemingly purposeful jabbing are simply an expression of their own biases and limiting beliefs of us and our capabilities. They ignore our boundaries because they themselves have none and they have the low self-esteem to prove it. But that's not to suggest they wish us harm. In fact, they're really just afraid.

Remember: The people who love and care for us the most don't want us to be happy, they want us to be safe.

But that's not to say that we should accept external judgment of our boundaries. Other peoples' responses to our boundaries are not what make our boundaries right or wrong. Other peoples' assessment of what is acceptable or appropriate have no bearing whatsoever on whether or not our values are being violated or protected. Do not accept other peoples' opinions about the validity or necessity of your boundaries, you're the only one who has to live with (or without) them.

For many of us and our identities happiness and safety are incongruent. In fact, our emotional needs profile can significantly affect the shape and size of our boundaries. For those of us who are certainty or growth driven, our independence is a key factor in the need for many strong boundaries. This can earn us a label of "difficult," "rigid," or "stubborn," but what's important is to live in alignment with our needs.

For others of us who are love & connection or uncertainty focused, boundaries feel like an impediment to the expression of our life's purpose and natural state. But believe it or not, the lack of boundaries is, in itself, a boundary. Knowing our limits and identity gives us the power to set intentional expectations of ourselves and those we choose to invite into our lives.

Most importantly, we must commit to honoring our values first with ourselves in order to congruently carry that forward into our other relationships. Being clear on your own importance and honoring your values as a matter of principle results in higher self-esteem, greater self-worth, and a more positive outlook in general.

Recognize that if we cannot honor our own values and needs we cannot expect anyone else to, either. Additionally, a person cannot give to others what they do not have within themselves. When one lacks self-esteem and self-worth, they cannot generously offer these traits to others nor will they respectfully honor others' boundaries.

Without internal boundaries, external conduct will be inconsistent and heavily influenced by mood and energy. The values of the individual are paramount to this "virtuous circle," because it is only when they are honored that a person can act unselfishly and with sincerity.

CHAPTER 8

Relationships

"The most painful thing is losing yourself in the process of loving someone too much, and forgetting that you are special too."

— Ernest Hemingway

Little of this book would matter if we each lived on that deserted island all by ourselves. Without external influence, we would have no other choice but to be our authentic selves. It's only when we interact with each other, jostle for status, and negotiate for shared resources that we start to compromise our values and needs.

Consider for a minute how complicated your thoughts and motivations are and then multiply that complexity exponentially simply by having to deal with other personalities with equally complicated motives and drivers. It's our interdependence and cooperation that really complicates our existence.

Relationships, whether they are with friends, family, or lovers are the grenades that get tossed into our psyches and cause us to doubt and second guess ourselves. Our need for connection and love tends to (seemingly) override all other influences of our behavior.

All of this is obviously worth the hassle. Accumulation of resources and status are senseless without a tribe to share them with. We are biologically driven to connect to and share our lives with others. Relationships inspire us to make sacrifices for the greater good, to strive to become better versions of ourselves, and pass on our experiences in the hopes that the next generation will rise even higher.

So how is it then that relationships can become toxic, painful, and even destructive to our authenticity and purpose?

FUSION

Most commonly, we received messages as children (long before we were legally authorized to accept the terms and conditions of the agreement) that the very meaning of life is to be accepted by others into a relationship. We have accepted that no matter what else we accomplish in life, the greatest measure of our worth is whether or not anyone loves us.

Whether it is being welcomed into a social circle or the corner office, we were made to believe that "success" in life would be measured by the achievement of certain titles: husband, wife, mother, father, executive vice president.

The pursuit of that status became an unchallenged belief and we (unconsciously) made it our prime directive. It became acceptable for us to suppress the desire for adventure or growth and knowledge, otherwise known as differentiation, if they did not serve the main goal of becoming socially successful through the attainment of these relationship titles. And we lost ourselves.

More dangerously, we naturally assumed that the person to whom we had committed ourselves was now responsible for our happiness, fulfillment, and identity. We learned growing up in a fused family structure that our purpose was to serve others, not ourselves. Certainly, it's perfectly natural and healthy to care for loved ones, but when neediness becomes power the dynamic becomes toxic.

Imagine the ideal I presented earlier about our primal drive to become a member of a group and the desire to attain status within that group. If the group in question is a fused family the way to be accepted into the group is to demonstrate how you can serve other members of the group. And then, where neediness is power, attaining status within the group is through perpetuating the cycle of relying on others to meet your (often unspoken, passive-aggressive) needs.

Yikes! It's no wonder the divorce rate climbs year after year.

When Eddie first reached out to me he was distraught; his wife wanted a divorce and he never saw it coming. He couldn't believe it—everything he did day in and day out was in an effort to meet her needs and now she was rejecting him!

When she was sick, he skipped work and cared for her. When she was sad, he would close the blinds and they would watch sad dramas together. When she was happy, he would pull himself out of his own funk and follow along gleefully. When she was mad at someone, he would jump on the bandwagon and point out all their flaws with her.

But when he was upset he never let it show. When he didn't agree with her, he let it go and swallowed his beliefs. When she rejected his advances or suggestions he chalked it up to bad timing or yet another way to put her needs ahead of his own. After all, why should he care where or when they ate dinner? Happy wife, happy life, right?

He knew they weren't as happy as they were when they met, but all marriages go through a patch and he made all the changes she ever asked of him. He stopped wasting time playing bass with his buddies, he dropped out of his Master's program when taking care of their two young children became a burden to her, and he accepted that sex was overrated.

Eddie was able to recount each of their recurring arguments with frightening accuracy. By his account it was because they had the same fight a million times without much resolution. They would yell and scream and stomp off, maybe slam a door, but in the morning or after several days of silence things would thaw and go back to normal.

At its worst he had suggested marriage counseling, but she vehemently refused, and cited that several of their friends had tried and it never made much difference. Besides, that was them and they needed outside help. When he suggested he would seek out some help from a men's coach she told him he was crazy and weak so he tried even harder to accept his faults and shortcomings.

Ultimately, Eddie learned not to trust his own thoughts, motives, or feelings without vetting them through his wife. When he confronted her about her suspected affair, he accepted that he had driven her to it by not adequately meeting her needs.

In a fused relationship, members believe they must respond to the needs and moods of the other, most often the negative moods. Each believes that caretaking equates to love and that when this can't be sustained over time or there is the perception of inequality there is no longer any love. Anger, resentment, and blame replace the affection and the relationship sours to the point of alienation.

The tension and anxiety within these dynamics are high. The worst possible offense you can commit in a fused relationship is to do anything to upset the other member or members. The mood of the relationship is dictated by the lowest common denominator of the most anxious and constrained member. Every other personality is expected to follow suit and limit their expression and individuality in kind.

All forms of expression are filtered through how the rest of the unit will respond or react. Mind reading becomes a required skill and we're notoriously bad at mind reading (FYI). We speculate, guess, ruminate, and otherwise drive ourselves crazy trying to meet everyone else's unspoken needs and desires while ignoring our own.

And all of this occurs while our own subconscious is trying desperately to meet our needs and live within our value set. Every action we take that is not in alignment with those needs and values creates internal tension and anxiety that eventually bubble over through self-destructive or antisocial outbursts. We lose our cool and explode or shut down and withdraw completely.

Relationships that persist within this framework tend to result in one catatonic member and one frantic overachiever. The overachiever both resents the catatonic one and works nonstop to change them. The catatonic member gives up all ambition and control to the other in the hopes that their compliance will result in at least some peace, but remains obsessed with the attainment of freedom without action.

Sound familiar?

Fused relationships are easily identifiable through some common traits:

- Constant fighting and bickering, but avoidance of conflict
- Little to no resolution of issues because resolution requires consensus
- Independence and autonomy are viewed as "bad" or "trouble-making" behavior

- Individuals may not excel, especially where enjoyment of success is concerned
- No one trusts or believes their own motives or needs
- No one is truly in charge, in fact, no one really knows who's doing what
- Members exhibit high levels of authority while accepting absolutely no responsibility

The best, and most dysfunctional example of this is the adage, "Happy wife, happy life." This is literally a socially accepted phrase that we all say tongue-in-cheek, but it exemplifies how we treat our relationships, specifically our romantic ones. It conditions us to accept that if we can make and keep someone else happy we have earned our happiness and it will be allowed. And if we can't, well, it's clearly our fault and we don't deserve to be happy, especially if other people around us aren't happy. Fusion personified.

Not only does this relinquish all responsibility and control of creating and pursuing our own happiness, but it also dumps a whole lot of responsibility on the other person (in this case the "wife"). I know firsthand that this dynamic is a downward spiral of stress and resentment. Not only is it no fun to be reliant on someone else for your own happiness, what about when everyone else's happiness is reliant on you and your mood?

When you have a bad day or just feel like you need a break you now have the shame of letting everyone else down with your "bad mood." That type of stress and response tends not to snap us out of a funk, it makes it worse. Also, when one family member is responsible for the tone and mood of the entire family it is exhausting! It's unfair to everyone.

DIFFERENTIATION

So, what's the alternative? Differentiation. Which, shouldn't surprise you, hinges on every member of a relationship having a clear identity and set of needs that they themselves are responsible for achieving. Crazy talk, I know, but bear with me.

Differentiation is the act of knowing and being yourself in the presence of and despite the presence of others.

Healthy differentiation of self is about being true to oneself while maintaining relationships with others. These relationships are important to the individual because they help them identify themselves and how they want to live their life. Differentiated relationships allow for people to grow and move forward in life while also positively impacting other peoples' lives.

This is different from unhealthy differentiation, which can cause people to feel like they don't belong or don't know who they are anymore, thus causing them distress and anxiety through a sense of isolation. The ability to differentiate oneself from another is necessary for healthy relationships. We must be able to maintain our own sense of identity when in a relationship with another person. This ability is necessary for both partners in a relationship, but it can prove difficult when you are in a situation with someone who has a borderline personality disorder.

Healthy Differentiation:

- Allows for growth and enrichment independently and together
- Eliminates the compulsion to compromise values and identity
- Deepens attachment through vulnerability and honesty

- Allows for healthy resolution of conflict
- Reduces the stress and anxiety surrounding the fear of rejection

It's easy to imagine being differentiated when times are good, but when we become stressed, especially in the face of conflict, we will quickly revert to fused behaviors without a firm understanding and belief of our true value. If our only measure of self-worth is of being in a relationship, any threat to that relationship is a threat to our identity.

NEW RELATIONSHIPS

Let's begin with an easy example—starting fresh! From this moment forward, every connection and relationship you establish should be modeled as a differentiated relationship.

It doesn't matter whether we're seeking new friends or the holy grail of relationships—true love—these rules apply to everyone we invite into our lives. If we're starting from scratch the best approach is to apply a few of the lessons we've already learned in previous chapters. Namely, defining our identity, writing our essay answers, and establishing our must haves and must nots.

First and foremost: scis te ipsum. Know thyself. Complete your values and needs work and really understand who you are and what you want from any connections you make. Intentionality is the name of the game, so next, write out your ideal outcome as your essay answer. Don't rely on the multiple-choice answers presented to you via an app based on the randomness of favorite bands, common high schools, or proclivity for tacos. These things do not exactly form a strong foundation for a relationship.

Finally, we have to break the cycle of believing we will accept whoever accepts us. Set relationship boundaries for yourself by establishing your must haves and must nots. Resist the urge to just write down all the ways you've been hurt in the past, "Must not lie, cheat, live with ex…." Those are fear and scarcity based needs.

Instead, use your values to define unacceptable attitudes and deal-breaking beliefs. Do not judge yourself, your answers are not a judgment of others, just a declaration of your needs and desires. You're just creating your wish list; not everyone will qualify and that's OK. Many of us start to resist these types of thoughts and requirements because we feel as though we're judging people. We're not. I don't care what you do with your life, but I do care how you impact mine.

If you can perform these three steps *before* going on the hunt and you hold yourself to these requirements, boundaries, and standards you're going to meet some pretty incredible people and you're going to be a better version of yourself for it.

OLD RELATIONSHIPS

I said that was the easy part. But how then do we handle or renegotiate existing relationships that were established and cultivated on fusion and/or an old version of who we were?

Section III of this book (just around the corner) is dedicated to the internal objections and obstacles you are going to face as you adopt these new ways of thinking and treating yourself, so put your doubt and objections aside for a few more pages and follow along.

The fact is that as an Identity & Purpose coach I have no predetermined outcome in mind for my clients, I can't. That is to say, I can't really limit myself to specific success criteria for a client other than pointing them in the right direction. My job in those sessions, and in this book, is to arm every client with the information and tools necessary to do what is best for them. My only goal here and there is to help you become the very best version of yourself possible.

OK, so, despite what inference you might make, I do not endorse marriage or relationships, nor do I think marriages and relationships are the end goal. Again, the end goal for me (and hopefully eventually for you) is for you to be the happiest, most fulfilled version of yourself possible. For some of you, that means finding the right person and creating an incredible life together. For others that may mean severing ties with some of the people from your past and going it alone.

For still others, it may mean casting aside just about everything you thought you wanted or needed to be happy and accepted, and instead rewriting the entire rule book.

So, regardless of the outcome, the steps are pretty similar to the above. Define your (independent) identity, write your essay answers, and establish your must haves and must nots. It's simple, but not easy. You are going to be heavily influenced by your current surroundings and existence if you can't set aside what you think the outcome is going to be if you answer a certain way.

Just because you admit to yourself that independence is your number one priority does not mean that your only course of action is to divorce your spouse and disown your kids. It may just require you to make new relationships, renegotiate existing relationships, and end some relationships that repeatedly violate that value.

If that scares you, keep reading and remember we're going to face objections together in the coming chapters. Don't focus on an outcome right now, just do the work. Pretend you are your own coach and detach from the expectation of outcome and the threat to your existing identity.

If you believe what I've shared about happiness and relationships then you also believe that the only true path to deep acceptance and intimacy is through differentiation and honesty. First with yourself, then with those you choose to invite into your life.

Denying or suppressing your true nature is like painting over rust—it only lasts for a little while before it comes back to the surface and makes everything ugly again.

COMMUNICATION

The undisputed king of relationship enders is poor communication. For a species that has grown and flourished based on its big brains' ability to synthesize, evaluate, and share information, we have become victims of our own success. We have created such sophisticated communication styles and methods that we are constantly miscommunicating.

This is another area that has thousands of its own books, but for our purposes, I'm going to talk about communicating through your emotional needs profile and using your partner's need to better communicate.

To do this you need to understand that we're all seeking safety and security in our relationships. Depending on your values and needs profile that safety and security may look different. Take for instance the difference of how a certainty driven person and an uncertainty driven person might interpret safety and security differently.

A certainty driven person would most likely view the expression of safety and security as having a routine, being reliable and consistent, and/or requiring lots and lots of detailed communication. Certainty is risk-averse and therefore the unknown is stressful and anxiety-inducing.

On the contrary, an uncertainty driven individual would seek safety and security through their own independence, spontaneity, and autonomy. Each of these drivers leads to less detail and more infrequent communications.

I used extreme examples to make a point. Imagine if these two people were trying to make plans together. Each person's need for safety and security would be highly threatened and they would have no idea why.

Frank called me from the road. He was late for dinner with his wife. He said he could picture her there, sitting at "their" table, checking and rechecking her watch, getting more and more frustrated by the minute. He knew he was in for it.

He was crafting his apology. He was just going to explain that starting and running his own business meant that sometimes, no matter how hard he tried, things required his input or presence. Things that only he could do wouldn't wait until tomorrow just because it was the second Wednesday of the month (date night). He had his calendar open, ready to show her the intricate details of every meeting and deadline he had that day.

He would apologize profusely and repeatedly all night and even show her his phone to prove how many calls he'd made and received all day working hard, for them, to get this business off the ground. She had to forgive him.

All that sounded very convincing and very justified, but she was still going to be pissed. She was still going to feel hurt and disappointed. Not because Frank was thoughtless or inconsiderate or didn't show her enough attention, but because none of that spoke to what was really hurting her.

Franks' wife was driven above all else by love & connection and his tardiness was taking away from her need to be connected to her husband. She had been looking forward to this dinner since last month's date because of how hard he had been working, not in spite of it.

But Frank was preparing the explanation that he would want to hear because Frank is contribution driven. His plea was going to be about how all the work he was doing, instead of being at dinner on time, was for the greater good, how it was in response to all the people, including her, that were counting on him to succeed.

Does the phrase "falling on deaf ears" mean anything to you?

When I asked Frank what the most important thing about date night was to his wife, he replied, "Being alone, just the two of us," and in that response was the answer to the question of how to apologize to her for the offense as she interpreted it.

In the end Frank decided it was best to apologize, sincerely, and acknowledge how his tardiness impacted their time together. He also felt it important to let her know that he wasn't late because she was less important to him than whatever kept him, but he was late because of how important she was to him and how he was working so hard to reflect that.

Finally, he would set his phone to "silent," put it in his pocket and give her his undivided attention for the rest of the night.

The first step to successfully communicating your needs is to know and understand your own drivers and communication preferences. Identity work is paramount to presenting yourself authentically and being clear on your needs. Specifically, in this instance, your communication needs. How do you need to receive information and feedback and how often?

One of the best skills we can learn and master in our lives is the ability to communicate the information we're trying to share in a format and structure that the receiver will best understand. We must accept that what we say is only a small fraction of what is conveyed. How we say it and, more importantly, how it's filtered and interpreted by the receiver have a significant impact on how the information is understood and what conclusions are drawn from it.

Take Pavlov's dog for example. The sound of a bell means food and therefore the dog's mouth waters. The dog had been conditioned to associate the sound of a bell with feeding time.

We hold thousands, tens of thousands, of these "conditions" inside our own minds. The key to effective communication is to understand that though we may each have been conditioned by a specific trigger, it does not mean we all share the same conditioned response.

Pavlov could have just as easily conditioned a second dog to associate the ringing of a bell with getting beaten by a stick.

So, where one family does not associate loud voices and cursing as a threat, another family absolutely does. As a result, what you think is normal may in fact be threatening the very safety and security of your partner.

That does not mean to suggest that we should spend our lives walking on eggshells worried that everything we do and say could be threatening everyone around us. What it does mean, though, is that we do have to be aware that even though we may think we're being very clear and direct, our message may not be received as intended.

The converse is true as well. We need to understand that we have a ton of internal biases that are filtering, organizing, and assessing every single message we receive. That is the seat of self-sabotage and confirmation bias.

If we believe we're incapable of attaining a certain goal, even the most supportive and encouraging message will be distorted to align with our internal narrative. "Good luck!," oh sure, because I need luck because I can't do this, because I've tried thirty times before and it's never worked out...good luck? Screw you.

Huh?

It's incredibly powerful to be able to use empathy in your communication especially when tensions are high, which they usually are in a close relationship. Being able to make an educated guess at what your partner's most influential emotional needs are will help you craft and deliver your message in a way that will be best received and understood.

If you know your partner is driven by love & connection, be sure that your communication is delivered in a way that honors that need and doesn't unintentionally threaten the safety and security of that connection.

Communication, and relationships in general, take a lot of practice and intention to keep healthy. First and foremost, though, you must put on your own oxygen mask. Fulfill your needs, protect your boundaries and don't let the need to be accepted by anyone influence the choices that will allow you to be accepted by the right ones.

SECTION III

Objections

CHAPTER 9

Beliefs

"The moment you doubt whether you can fly, you cease forever to be able to do it."

— J. M. Barrie, Peter Pan

One of the most frustrating parts of my journey of self-improvement was the constant obstacle of context. An author would put forth a concept or suggestion and something inside me would immediately find reasons (excuses!) why it wouldn't work for me or didn't apply to me because of my specific situation.

It was frustrating because most authors and coaches glossed right over the very obvious issue of objections and it was frustrating because why would I spend the time and effort of buying and reading a book and course only to dismiss the advice within?

The irony of that whole situation is that it isn't the information within books that we're seeking, it's the belief. We want to hear about the author's struggle, their hero's journey, in the hopes that something inside us will shift and compel us into action. Action that had in the past eluded us.

The lack of knowledge isn't what holds us back. We have access to the entirety of all collected human knowledge within our pockets. We know what to eat and what not to eat, yet we are unhealthy and overweight. We know how much to save and how to budget and yet we carry more unsecured debt than ever before. We have the ability to access, communicate (in hundreds of languages), and connect with nearly every other human on the planet and yet we are more isolated and lonely than ever before.

Knowledge is not the barrier anymore, belief is. Our ability to accept that our behavior is the culmination of a complex collection of experiences and decisions is the key to changing our outcomes. And the number one factor in the rationale behind our choices is belief.

The belief that we're always going to be out of shape, broke, and alone is not based on reality, but on the expectations that were placed on us by our tribe's inherited beliefs. Of all the things we pass down from one generation to the next, our belief systems are the ones that are most universally unchallenged.

Typically, when we're faced with an internal struggle or challenge, an unscratchable itch in our minds, or an imperceptible calling we instinctively change our external surroundings. We move, change jobs, we break up, and start over. It never occurs to us that the conflict is internal.

As I've outlined several times so far, the anxiety and stress we feel in our lives is most often due to the violation of a nonnegotiable personal value, not the noisy neighbor or cranky boss. It's deeper, bigger, more fundamental to the very fabric of our belief system.

The internal conflict is caused by a choice or circumstance wherein we have chosen to violate our own values and needs on a daily basis without any form of reconciliation or compensation... because we believe we're doing the right thing. The craziest part is we're usually in complete control of the conflict.

When a child chooses to go to their parent's alma mater to study a particular subject because of its safe, secure future instead of going to The International Stunt School (swear to God that's a real thing!) to honor their need for adventure, they have created an unresolved conflict that will not just go away. And they did it not because they didn't know any better, but because they believed they were doing the right thing.

That's an obvious example, but a more insidious example is the choice we make, not because we think we're making a good choice, but because we believe we *can't* do something. Those are self-limiting beliefs. I know we use the term a lot, but self-limiting beliefs need to be thoroughly understood if you hope to reveal your true identity and purpose.

Self-limiting beliefs are actually beliefs you've adopted that you don't really believe. They prevent you from living your truth because they conflict with your values and needs. If you value adventure and need uncertainty, but you were raised to accept that adventure and uncertainty are too risky, are life-threatening, and will leave you broke and destitute, you will make decisions that deny those values and needs.

When Gerry was little his mom was always concerned for his safety. Helmets, reflective clothes, and being home before dark were nonnegotiable laws. So when he received a brand new Diamondback BMX bike for his birthday he couldn't believe his luck. Finally, he would be able to ride the trails around his neighborhood with all his friends!

But when his mom said he could only ride it in the driveway, he was heartbroken. Talk about keeping your prized stallion in the stable. To be fair though, he knew that kids got hurt all the time. Broken wrists, lacerations...his friends were covered with scabs and scars. Really cool scabs and scars.

Eventually Gerry grew bolder and one of his favorite things to do was to sneak out and ride his bike to his neighbor's where the rules surrounding safety were, let's just say, "looser." He learned to ride faster and harder than ever before and he loved it.

These escapes became a normal part of growing up and so did the shame and guilt of defying his mother's wishes. Gerry began to associate his desire for adventure with shame and irresponsibility. He believed that only bad, immature people did risky or challenging things.

Once, when I asked him about his plans for the weekend (specifically ways he planned to honor his value of adventure), he said, "I was going to ride my motorcycle to the beach, but the weather's kind of sketchy and I think they said the traffic was going to be bad, so it's probably best to just stay close to home."

As we talked more about his decision, it became clear that it was not that he was afraid and had inherited his mother's risk aversion. In fact he communicated quite the opposite response, where risk and adventure had become tantalizing taboos for him, and the thrill associated not only with the physical acts, but the emotional rebellion, fueled him.

He had, though, internalized the belief that only children craved risk and adventure and that at some point you have to grow up and put those things aside. But he didn't believe it.

For years, Gerry suppressed his need for fun and excitement to pursue his (very safe) career. He went to work on time and came straight home after (usually arriving home before dark). He planned, and scheduled, and carefully weighed risks and devised contingencies for every event in his life. And he was bored to tears.

When Gerry finally sat down to write out his beliefs around adventure and excitement he couldn't believe how directly they violated his values. He knew (rationally) that he wanted, needed!, adventure in his life, that he wanted to explore the world and all its wonders, but he talked or planned himself out of doing it every time!

It wasn't that he had inherited a faulty set of values, it's that he had accepted a set of beliefs that his values were bad, irresponsible, and immature. But those weren't really his beliefs, they were his mom's. Today Gerry has tons of adventures and has accepted that, even though his mom was just trying to protect him, her beliefs around risk and adventure were not his own.

You created that dynamic because you forced yourself to believe and do something that is contrary to your very purpose. Remember what I said about the people who love and care for us the most: They don't want us to be happy, they want us to be safe. And being safe doesn't give a crap about your authentic identity and purpose, it only cares about your survival. If you bought, borrowed, or (better yet) stole this book you don't want to just survive, you are desperate to thrive!

So, are you being influenced by inherited and self-limiting beliefs? Yes. Damn straight you are. Any time you've tried to make a change in your life and you gradually gave up or rationalized away the effort, you were impacted by the belief that you didn't have it in yourself to achieve the goal. It was not a lack of knowledge, resources, or tools it was your belief that you shouldn't, couldn't, or didn't deserve the results that stopped you.

But that's not to say you should feel shame about that. In fact, one of the first things you need to do is forgive yourself for the failures of the past because now you know that it was you all along. You were fighting your instinctual need to belong to a group by conforming to the group's rules and culture. By staying warm and safe in the bosom of acceptance you were choosing to stay right where you are.

Breaking free from one group to pursue admission into another is frightening and daunting, but the greatest motivator in the world is knowing that you're doing it to honor your authentic gifts and purpose. And, ironically, acceptance is just on the other side of authenticity.

OK, so how do we assess and tackle our self-limiting and flat-out wrong beliefs?

Firstly, you're probably completely unaware of most of those beliefs. They have always been there, they're part of your source code, part of your language, part of your routine, part of your dreams, and part of your fears. So, you need to identify them.

EXERCISE 11

A great start is to grab your trusty journal and label a couple of adjacent pages with titles like, "I always..." and "I never..." and then start writing. Don't filter, don't think, don't judge, just write. When you fill the page you're going to have a really good idea of all the ways you limit your choices and options in life just based on what you were taught to believe is right, wrong, acceptable, and approved.

As bonus work (for all my approval seekers) start a couple more pages with more specific titles like, "I could never...," "I would never...," "I have never...," and "I have always...." Play with these subtle variations until you unlock your particular brand of denial and adopted beliefs.

Some of us are so programmed not to step out of line that we'll even manipulate the questions so the answers don't violate the belief. You have no chance of ever being honest and authentic with others if you can't first be honest and authentic with yourself. Start there.

Once you have a decent amount of "beliefs" captured, go back and ask yourself if *you* really believe those things. We've managed to break a lot of stereotypes and prejudices in this world by questioning what we were told was true. We used to believe lightning was caused by angry gods, that disease was caused by evil spirits, and that only birds can fly.

It's time to challenge all the antiquated beliefs you have about yourself.

When I was separated from my children I believed I was the worst father in the world...because I was told time after time that to be a good father I had to be there for them, all the time, every day, every night. But confronted with the impossibility of my situation I had to really challenge my beliefs around what it means to *me* to be a good father.

Presence is important, yes, but more important to me were my beliefs that a good father empowers his children through support and encouragement. Well, thanks to Tim Cook I was able to do that from 1847 miles away as often as if I were in the same house. I relieved myself of the guilt and shame and focused on what being a positive influence in my kids' lives really meant.

Because of that, I am closer to my kids now than I ever was by taking credit for a horrible shallow metric like presence, and instead I concentrate on doing what I think is truly valuable to them which is living by example and being conscious of the unintended limiting beliefs I may be inadvertently passing down to them. I also make it a point to ensure they're doing what makes them happy even if it's not what's best for me.

But I had to start by challenging the expectations and success measures I blindly adopted from my parents and teachers, many of which are horribly outdated and even harmful. According to Darwin's *On the Origin of Species*, it is not the most intellectual of species that survives; it's not the strongest that survives; it is the species that is best able to adapt and adjust to its changing environment that survives and flourishes.

A rigid belief system that does not account for your individuality and changing circumstances will not only limit your potential, but your ability to thrive and provide for those around you. Recognizing that your beliefs and values are closely intertwined gives you awareness of and control of your choices and ultimately your entire environment.

Our beliefs are the engine that drives our identity. If we believe bad things about ourselves and we make bad choices because of those beliefs then we perpetuate and solidify those beliefs. Additionally, if we believe something bad about ourselves and we make a choice that conflicts with that belief and we fail to achieve the desired outcome, that can serve as confirmation bias and we're less likely to challenge those beliefs in the future.

Unfortunately, as powerful as confirmation bias is, it is a lagging indicator of our true self-worth and success and it is susceptible to our own interpretation. Far too many people judge their outcomes as a comparison to other peoples' results and thereby limit their potential.

This is a great place to challenge your "I've always…" or "I've never…" beliefs. Confirmation bias draws all its power from the past. But as we know, past success or failure is not an indication of future results. Basically, don't believe that you can't change, grow, or learn.

This brings me to my final point about beliefs and that is the difference between capacity and willingness. It is a very different thing to be incapable of an action than to be unwilling to even try. Far too many times a client or friend will say, "Oh, I can't do that," when what they really mean is "Oh, I'm not going to do that."

When you tell yourself you can't do something, because you were told you couldn't or because you believe you can't, you are choosing the limitation. Recognizing the difference between ability and willingness is a necessary step in changing your life's path and outcome.

I'm fairly confident that a lot of the things you've accepted in your life are actually the result of a limiting belief and not of your inability to change them. That's about as tough as my love is going to get in this book. I'm not interested in shaming any of you into making changes, I don't believe in negative reinforcement or motivation as a means to compel change.

In fact, I believe quite the opposite. I'm writing this book to encourage and empower you to shed the limitations in your life that you've accepted on blind faith and instead create a life that is both extremely exciting and incredibly satisfying without changing who you are, but instead changing what you believe.

CHAPTER 10

Fear & Consequences

"Nothing in life is to be feared, it is only to be understood. Now is the time to understand more, so that we may fear less."

— Marie Curie

I'm guessing you expect me to give you the same old psycho-babble about how to abolish your fear and live life completely untethered. Well, I'm not. Fear is a useful, powerful, necessary force in our lives. We all need to heed its warnings and trust our instincts. It's only when our fears interfere with our ability to live in alignment with our values and fulfill our needs that it needs to be addressed.

Our fear has evolved over millennia to protect us and our resources from harm. Fear lets us know that we've forgotten something, underestimated something, or failed to properly prepare for something. But fear can also prevent us from doing what we know is risky, but necessary.

Natural fear is a fear that an organism has innately or instinctively to protect itself from harmful events. An example of natural fear is the sensation of fearing heights, which is an instinct because a fall can lead to death. A learned fear, on the other hand, is something that one learns to be afraid of through experience. For example, an individual might have been attacked by a dog when they were young and then learned to be afraid of all dogs.

We all have a fear of something. It's a natural part of being human. But some fears can be debilitating and can affect your everyday life. These fears are called phobias and they may be the result of an anxiety disorder or stress disorder. One such common phobia is social anxiety which is the fear of being judged by other people in social situations ranging from speaking to large groups to meeting new people.

But just because you may have a fear of public speaking does not in itself demand that you face and conquer that fear. If you can be happy and live your life's highest purpose without ever having to speak in front of a large crowd, why put yourself through the drama and stress of abolishing the fear without just cause?

Natural fears are instincts that are passed down from generation to generation so they are deeply ingrained in our culture. Learned fears are things that are learned over time through experience or exposure. To allow yourself to be authentic and realize your true purpose, you need to be able to recognize and overcome the fears that are trapping you in your current dysfunctional or limiting identity.

As I said, fear is useful and powerful as long as it is not crippling or preventing you from becoming the best version of yourself. It has been my experience that clients who felt a particular fear were not properly motivated and the fear became too large to handle.

The fears that we're concerned with, in the context of your journey, though, are the fears of abandonment, disapproval, and detachment. These are the emotional fears that prevent you from making the changes necessary to pursue and accept your true identity.

Each of these fears could be experienced as a fear of failure or a fear of success. In failure we fear the ridicule or judgment of others. In success we fear being found out or finding we've overestimated ourselves.

Fear of Failure Looks Like:	Fear of Success Looks Like:
• Analysis-Paralysis	• Self-Sabotage
• Procrastination	• Halfway In
• Need to Escape	• Disbelief
• Rumination Over Past	• Goal Addiction

One fear you may be feeling since you picked up this book is the fear that if you're successful in determining your life's true identity and purpose and actually pursue it that you're going to disappoint those around you. That you're going to *have* to change a bunch of things about yourself, or that it's going to be extremely difficult to make the changes necessary to live in alignment with that identity and purpose.

I can attest that from the moment I accepted my true identity, my life and choices have become easier, more fulfilling, and positively reinforcing. The only people I have lost or disappointed were those who were benefiting from my low self-esteem, approval-seeking, and/or other toxic behaviors. And I don't need them in my life. (I would highlight that if I were you.)

Regardless of which fear you're experiencing, most peoples' attempts to abolish their fears fail because they rely on wildly ineffective tactics like willpower, negative reinforcement (such as shame), or mimicry of someone else's success. Blech. As I touched on in Chapter 5, positive reinforcement is the only way to go, and it's more fun!

Make no mistake, if you think determining your true identity and purpose in life has to be a miserable slog wherein you turn your entire life upside down, lose all your friends and family, and start over from scratch, you're wrong.

In fact, positive psychology is a new field that studies the factors that contribute to happiness and well-being. It is an applied branch of psychology, which helps people to overcome their fears, find motivation and achieve success through acts of positive reinforcement.

Positive psychology has been proven to be effective in every facet of our lives. It can help us achieve our goals by getting rid of our fears. So if we want to motivate ourselves to act, we should assess what kind of approach would work for us best—either "doing" or "faking it."

One of the most important steps you can take and skills you must learn to finally take control of your fear is how to meet and satisfy your own emotional needs. Breaking the cycle of relying on an external source or single person to meet your emotional needs is empowering and extremely healthy.

According to Buddha, the basic cause of all human suffering is **"the attachment to the desire to have** (craving) **and the desire not to have** (aversion)". Attainment and loss. But the fear of detachment is merely the impression that we will not be able to "get" what we need or that we will "lose" what we already have.

By learning how to create healthy self-care activities that meet our needs we overcome both fears because we teach ourselves that we alone are responsible for and capable of "getting" and "keeping" everything we need and want.

It is only then that we can confidently take responsibility for our own happiness and invite people into our lives to experience it with us as opposed to inviting people into our lives in the hopes that they, or something they possess, will bring us happiness, acceptance, love, connection, or whatever else it is we're seeking.

One of the trickiest things our minds do to protect us, though, is to hide our fears from us. A subconscious fear is a feeling of intense and irrational fear in the absence of any external threat. There might be multiple reasons for this kind of feeling, but generally, we experience it as a sense of constant anxiety.

Anxiety is a natural reaction to fear. It's important to understand the difference between the two because anxiety can be treated with therapy, medication, or both. There are many different stress management techniques that are available to help you deal with your stress. You can use them alone or combine them for more benefits.

You may find it helpful to first move your stress from inside to outside yourself. Try breathing exercises, think about what triggered your anxiety, practice a short meditation, take deep breaths, do yoga poses or take a walk around the block.

The point to this, though, is to ultimately seek the root cause of your fear through an assessment of your values and needs. Be honest and gentle with yourself, don't assign any shame or blame, but allow yourself to honestly accept and name your fear.

───────── **EXERCISE 12** ─────────

This is where I recommend that you play Powerball or Castaway. Depending on your particular mindset you may choose to pretend you've just won the Powerball or that you've washed up on a deserted island. Whichever you choose, the point of the exercise is to allow yourself to be completely honest about your feelings without fear of judgment.

If you were suddenly rich beyond your dreams or did not have to answer to anyone else, what would you honestly admit to yourself about your fears and needs?

Recognize that any significant fear will ultimately fall into one of the two categories above: fear of attainment or fear of loss. Next, determine if that fear is specific to a person or role in your life such as the approval of a parent or acceptance by a loved one.

Finally, create a healthy substitute to achieve that need (either fully or in part) and reduce your fear, stress, and anxiety surrounding it. I call this a Make-Before-Break strategy because you're making a healthy replacement before breaking a negative or toxic attachment.

As we discussed in Chapter 5, our likelihood of repeating a behavior has a lot to do with what happens to us when we take an action. Positive consequences have a stronger long-term influence than negative consequences. Whether positive or negative, consequences that happen immediately following an action with a high level of certainty are more likely to result in repeated behaviors too. These consequences are referred to as PICs and NICs. Positive-Immediate-Certain and Negative-Immediate-Certain.

If you're looking to change your behavior you have to ensure the new consequences are PICNICs.

But positive consequences alone won't necessarily get you where you want to be; for that you need to set reasonable goals. This is another area where I think common convention misses the mark and does a horrible disservice to us mortals.

Goal setting is easy, goal achievement is another story. Even after we overcome our fears of failure and success there are a lot of pitfalls and obstacles preventing us from achieving our goals. A necessary concept to accept is that obstacles and setbacks are not confirmation that you don't deserve to have what you want, they're just a natural side effect of the universe not really thinking about what you're doing.

What derails most people from their goals is that they fail to plan for inevitable setbacks and course corrections. Like other decision-making, setting goals needs to start with careful alignment to your values and needs and then a detailed "essay" answer approach to defining the outcome. This approach has been overly-simplified by saying you should "start with why."

What's worse is that you already know what's going to distract or discourage you and instead of planning for it, preparing for it, or mitigating it you use the inevitable setback as confirmation bias to support your fear and allow you to stay right where you are.

You have inherent strengths, weaknesses, and well established threats. None of these needs to be avoided. Success comes not from the absence of these things, but in the acceptance of them. By rationally acknowledging your challenges you can avoid an overly emotional response to future challenges.

Making a plan early and before you embark on your pursuit gives you the opportunity to think clearly and in perspective of the weight of the goal and the realistic magnitude of various obstacles. Thinking these things through avoids overreaction based on the emotion of the challenge.

A minor setback can become a dealbreaker if you're already tired, stressed, or worn down. If you drive blindly forward toward your goal fueled only by willpower and the promise to yourself that "this time will be different" without actually doing anything differently, you're setting yourself up for disappointment and failure.

This just perpetuates the cycle of shame and sense of failure as you reaffirm your fear that you "can't do it," "never could," or "always fail." The best way to guard against this is to remove those obstacles or devise a plan before you even set out. Self-sabotage is just another way of saying you are fully aware of how you will fail and you take no action to prevent it. If you're serious about achieving a goal, even one you've failed to achieve multiple times before, take specific steps to address your past failures so they don't impede you again.

 GOAL TRACKER:
therealcharlesbrowne.com/resources

Just as with defining yourself through your values and emotional needs, taking steps to assure your success requires that you take personal responsibility for the outcome of your choices and actions. Naming and planning for your setbacks sends a clear message to your subconscious that you are in control of your state, your choices, and your reality.

As you do this and achieve one goal after another you'll notice that your fears naturally become smaller and fewer. The more power you take back from your fears of attainment and loss the more peace and happiness you will experience.

CHAPTER 11

Emotional Pacifiers

"All work is the avoidance of harder work."

— *James Richardson*

We spend so much time and effort avoiding thoughts, feelings, and activities that cause us distress or discomfort that we can actually create more anxiety in the process. Fear and anxiety are often used as interchangeable words and we usually think that they mean the same thing. However, they are different and we should use them in different contexts.

Both fear and anxiety refer to a mental state of apprehension about future events, but the difference lies in the intensity and source of those feelings. Fear is characterized as an intense short-term emotion in response to a physical threat while anxiety is characterized as a less intense long-term emotional state (e.g., those related to psychological threats).

I know there are exceptions, but please bear with me.

Anxiety is a feeling of worry, unsettledness, or unease that makes us feel like we can't cope in any situation. This isn't intended to be a deep dive into anxiety disorders, but we do need to discuss how our fears and anxieties affect our behaviors. Specifically in this context, how we use unhealthy or destructive avoidance behaviors to soothe those fears and anxieties.

For our purposes, I'm going to be writing about anxiety, stress, and fear as they relate to challenges to our identity, safety, and security. It's important to establish healthy coping mechanisms in order to stop this negative cycle from happening over and over again.

The first tip is to know your triggers. Knowing what causes your anxiety can help you become more aware of when you are in an anxious state, and it will give you the opportunity to try different methods for stopping the anxiety attack before it gets worse. Or to employ healthy, positive self-care activities to abate those negative feelings.

In my work with clients (and myself), we talk about the difference between our authentic self, as we defined in Section I of this book, and the identity we were assigned by our parents, environment, and various group cultures. When we feel anxiety it is most often caused by the conflict between who we know ourselves to be and who we're trying to be.

When our assigned identity causes us to suppress our own needs or violate our (supposedly) nonnegotiable values we sense that as anxiety. Sometimes that anxiety is very apparent, but most times it's subtle and almost chronic, meaning it's *always* there.

Ideally, your ultimate goal is to be as authentic to your identity as possible. In a perfect existence, you would never experience the type of anxiety I'm describing because you would be in a perpetual state of alignment and authenticity. As I've stated, though, I'm not an idiot; I know that's very difficult if not impossible especially early in your journey. And when we feel that anxiety we work very hard to dissipate it through what I've come to call "emotional pacifiers."

Imagine a scenario where a person with the need for love & connection is deprived of that need by the dysfunction of their fused family environment. The need doesn't go away, it's still there, unresolved and unmet. That unfulfilled need is felt "like a splinter in your mind."

The stress, disappointment, yearning, and anxiety build nonstop. This is where our subconscious can be an unstoppable force as it works to resolve and soothe our anxiety by *any means necessary,* healthy or otherwise.

This is where a perfectly natural and healthy need can lead to unhealthy, even destructive behaviors. Your subconscious doesn't care one bit about your hopes, dreams, goals, or what's socially acceptable, it only cares that you're stressed and stress burns calories and threatens your continued survival.

So it does exactly what it's supposed to do: it grinds away at the problem until it finds or creates a solution. Your rational mind be damned. This can be observed as habitual, even obsessive behaviors like:

- Surfing Social Media
- Mindlessly Snacking
- Habitual Drinking
- Escaping in Pornography
- Compulsively Masturbating
- Impulse Shopping

- Rearranging Your Environment
- Endless To-Do Lists/Busywork

Basically, any activity that can distract your subconscious from the real unmet need or unresolved conflict. I also refer to these behaviors as emotional sugar or emotional carbohydrates because they are empty emotional calories that only provide short-term relief and are frequently followed by an emotional "crash" that perpetually restarts the cycle.

Emotional pacifiers come in many sizes and styles and are highly personalized based on your specific needs profile, values violation, and preferences, but they all have one thing in common: they're hiding unresolved unmet needs.

Their purpose is to provide us with the external attention, reassurance, validation, and acceptance we're not getting from our life. Which would be fine if they weren't hurting us, but typically, they are. Whether the damage is to our livers or our self-esteem, emotional pacifiers create an unhealthy dynamic in which we feel useless, unloved, unworthy, and ashamed.

Emotional pacifiers perpetuate their own cause which is that the messages we receive about our needs being unrealistic or unworthy are correct. Emotional pacifiers are a form of confirmation bias and they feed our self-limiting and self-sabotaging beliefs.

In a more tangible sense, emotional pacifiers prevent us from achieving our ideal physical, emotional, even financial states by engaging us in activities and habits that undermine the goals our rational brains have set for us.

That further deepens the toxic shame and feelings of power-lessness by making us believe that we lack the willpower to accomplish even the most basic goals. Knowledge is not the obstacle, we know how to lose weight, save money, and create businesses; emotional pacifiers are the obstacle.

Their false sense of security makes us feel like our needs are being met, that we're worthy and accepted, that we belong to and have status within our groups, but they lie. Emotional pacifiers are an avoidance technique we've created to convince ourselves that we're doing everything we can and that we're just unlucky or lack the skills and willpower to create a better reality.

And because of their temporary nature, emotional pacifiers keep us trapped in a cycle of seeking a quick fix and relief to our anxiety even though we know the better, long-term solution is to deal with our fears head-on. This is where our subconscious tricks us once again.

Let's face it, your subconscious is dumb. (Chill out, everybody's is.) It has a very basic set of rules and guidelines it operates by. First, it will ask, are you still alive? If yes, then don't move! Don't change anything because even if you're unfulfilled and miserable, at least you're alive!

This is a classic case of a risk avoidance survival technique, and choosing the devil you know rather than taking a chance on the devil you don't know seems like sound logic to your subconscious. If you're alive, no matter how uncomfortable you are, your subconscious is doing its job.

Second, it will ask, do we believe that? This is how and why affirmations don't work for most of us. Affirmations are, by their nature, an attempt to lie to ourselves and convince our subconscious to believe something that is patently false. "I am a multimillionaire." Good luck with that.

When we apply emotional pacifiers to ease an internal tension, we are allowing our subconscious to avoid risk and threats to our current status. Sounds nice, sounds harmless except when we ourselves have decided that the risk is worth the reward or that we can no longer tolerate the anxiety and violation of living in conflict with our true identities.

This section is here because if you've clearly outlined your true self then you alone are going to be the biggest obstacle to living in alignment with that identity. Residual self-identity, the comfort and familiarity of your old identity, is going to cause your subconscious to fight to keep you right where you are. Most commonly, through employing emotional pacifiers to convince you that it's "not that bad," or that "it's too late to change."

OK, I think I've made my point. We have emotional pacifiers working constantly in the background to pacify our anxiety, but they're actually not resolving their own root cause and therefore they're working against us to keep us stuck in the cycle of unmet needs and low self-esteem.

On to the good stuff—what do we do about it?

EXERCISE 13

First, like all of your work, take an assessment of how you specifically are being impacted. Grab a blank page and reflect or be aware over the next couple of days and note anytime you recognize anything that could be categorized as an emotional pacifier or avoidant behavior.

Resist the urge to judge yourself or immediately "fix" the behavior. Denying yourself from engaging in any soothing behaviors without first establishing a healthy replacement behavior can actually throw gasoline on the fire. We cannot endure unresolved anxiety for long before our subconscious will intervene to protect us.

This harkens back to my point that willpower is stupid. I've watched far too many people try to modify their own behavior through "willpower" and the result is typically a catastrophic failure with an overreaction back to old habits with devastating consequences.

Once you've identified a number of habits or compulsions that you know aren't really serving you or aren't healthy, work to identify which need or violation you think they might be trying to resolve. If you spend an exorbitant amount of time or assign an unreasonable amount of value to inane measures of your worthiness, such as "likes" for example, you may be yearning for love & connection or significance.

Additionally, you can pay particular attention to your compulsory behavior after a specific confrontation or perceived rejection to establish a direct cause and effect relationship. For example, if your lover or spouse rejects your sexual advances and you immediately turn to porn as an escape to ease the pain of rejection, the association is quite clear.

Do not judge yourself, just notice the behaviors.

> **NOTE: I am not a doctor. The information in this publication is not intended or implied to be a substitute for professional medical advice, diagnosis or treatment. You should always consult a licensed health care provider before beginning any dietary or fitness program.**

When I began evaluating my emotional pacifying behaviors I recognized early that the underlying issue was that I had been programmed to immediately work to alleviate any nervousness or anxiety with avoidant or replacement behaviors.

Anytime I felt stressed, challenged, or otherwise threatened I would instinctively revert to a soothing behavior. Not all of it was harmful or regressive, but the fact that I was uncomfortable with being uncomfortable was an indication to me that it was a limiting behavior. The first replacement techniques I mulled were based in exposure therapy, which loosely means doing what make you uncomfortable.

Aside from being nervous about that, I also thought it was stupid. I categorize most exposure techniques alongside affirmations in that they rely on gathering up an unreasonable amount of faith and willpower. I've firmly established that reliance on either is unreliable at best.

In my opinion and experience, though, what really was a better option than all that was to simply employ "pattern interrupts." What bothered me most about my emotional pacifiers is that they were so damn unconscious. I didn't like the fact that I was basically a lab rat for my subconscious.

I wanted to be in control of my state, in control of my responses to make better choices. I was confident that all I really needed was a split second to allow my conscious, rational brain to engage and that would go a long way towards eliminating the majority of my pacifying habits.

I found the thread of a solution during a yoga video with my man Tony Horton (creator of P90X). During one of his P90X One on One videos, Fountain of Youth, Tony is asked about the mental/emotional benefits of regular yoga practice.

His response was as follows, "The vast majority of Americans don't like yoga because they have to be calm in an isometric posture that is uncomfortable. It is working on joints, and ligaments, and tendons, and muscles, and patience, and breath. It's an atypical exercise, but I'll tell you if there's any society that needs it more than any other in the world, it's America."

In that moment I came to recognize that by learning to breathe through the discomfort of yoga I was actually learning to accept being uncomfortable. When muscles begin to burn our immediate instinct is to stand up, move or otherwise relieve the stress. I realized that is the physical equivalent of an emotional pacifier.

By choosing to stay in a pose I was demonstrating to my subconscious that, even though I was uncomfortable I was not in danger or threatened. I knew going in that I was going to be uncomfortable, but it was for my own good and I would emerge better for it.

The next technique I employed to train myself to better handle discomfort was intermittent fasting. It was only after several weeks of practice, though, that I made the association with emotional pacifiers. Fasting is a great, private way to develop and practice self-control.

I used fasting as a means to get comfortable with being uncomfortable. To this day I still consider yoga and fasting essential elements of my self-care routine.

If you're especially stuck here (you little angel) approach this from the opposite angle and start by reading through your emotional needs profile. How do you currently meet or fulfill those needs? What satisfies those needs in you?

PRO TIP: If you're not sure if a behavior is an emotional pacifier or healthy self-care, consider that emotional pacifiers only treat the effect, whereas healthy self-care serves the cause.

Also, assess your behavior over time. What may have started innocently enough could very well have, over time, swelled into a full-blown compulsion or unhealthy emotional pacifier. Look back over your social media history and take a look at your posts, pictures, and tone. Has it escalated, become more and more risque or confrontational?

If so, you're likely compelled by the attention or (apparent) approval you're receiving. You're driven by the superficial status and rush of whichever of your needs is being met. Left unchecked, you will abandon any other means to fulfillment for this emotional "sugar."

Zooming out on your life is a powerful tool for you to get a better perspective of how your habits have changed, sometimes imperceptibly, over time. I often say that we are in the eye of our own hurricane and we need to change our focus or perspective to really see what's going on around us.

As we discussed in Chapter 2, your top two emotional needs are those that are most important to you and therefore are the most likely focus of your pacifiers. Since they are the biggest buckets of needs in your life, they naturally require the most attention and diverse fulfillment strategies.

It's very unlikely that you're reading this book with completely filled emotional needs buckets. As such, you've very likely developed or are engaged in some pacifying behaviors to supplement your "organic" fulfillment sources.

Most people, unaware that these forces are at work within them, rely exclusively on just that—external, fate-driven fulfillment of their needs. As we discussed, we predominantly received messages early in life that the fulfillment of our needs was dependent on the whim and will of those responsible for our care.

Because of that message, we have grown to blindly accept that the fulfillment of our needs is the responsibility of others and is outside of our control. Nothing could be further from the truth. Not only are we alone responsible for the fulfillment of our needs, but we have the greatest potential to fulfill them.

So, the vast majority who are waiting for the people around them to meet their unspoken needs rely on emotional pacifiers, psychological junk food, to sustain them. The side effects of those choices are lives filled with resentment, stress, and longing.

To address our needs in a healthy and intentional way we need to replace our emotional pacifiers and passive-aggressive fulfillment techniques with healthy and positive practices that we control. To overcome our fears of loss and abandonment we need to design and administer our own self-care and answer our own needs.

Only then, when we can comfort our own anxiety, can we feel the peace and confidence of being personally responsible for our own happiness and care. When we've accomplished this we can then invite others to share in our lives with a clear conscience assured we're not seeking approval, validation, or permission from anyone but ourselves.

That's not to say all pacifiers need to be abolished or replaced. It is your life and therefore only you can determine if any of your choices and behaviors are impeding your progress or the achievement of your life's purpose. Just because I've called out a particular habit as an emotional pacifier doesn't make it inherently bad or wrong. Clearly, there's nothing unhealthy or destructive about cleaning out your garage, unless you're doing it as a means to avoid a larger issue...every two weeks.

Finally, when our needs are consistently being met in healthy and intentional ways we can once again revisit our emotional pacifiers if any still persist, and once again examine their root cause and work to erase them from our lives. I truly believe all "bad" behavior stems from fear and therefore any destructive behaviors that remain are the result of fear.

Addressing and facing these fears will allow us to determine how perpetuating these fears is serving us, and through challenging our beliefs and creating healthy self-care we can overcome them in order to be the best possible versions of ourselves.

CHAPTER 12

Guilt, Shame & Regret

"Show me a man who has never made a mistake, and I will show you one who has never tried anything."

— Albert Einstein

The trifecta of a wasted life lies in these three feelings. Of all other barriers to success, none of them comes close to competing with the amount of time and potential wasted feeling guilty, ashamed, or regretful. But knowing and accepting that they are the only things standing between us and a happy and fulfilled life are two very different things.

The most dangerous side effect of these emotions is that once we accept their judgment we rarely revisit or appeal the decision. We use them as confirmation bias for every decision thereafter. They are an emotion based on a belief caused by an interpretation established by an expectation and as such, they are fragile and subjective. And they are not law.

As I've stated several times throughout this book, we and we alone are responsible for the satisfaction of our needs and the control of our state. Our culture is littered with countless stories of people in much worse situations than our own who somehow magically picked themselves up, dusted themselves off, and created opportunity and success despite their past failures or limitations.

Our culture has an equal number of stories about people who, after the smallest of mistakes or errors, toss their lives away through inaction by ruminating on that single failed act, never allowing themselves to recover or move forward.

But the truth of what really happens to us is more nuanced because the majority of us don't live in those extreme cases, we live somewhere in the normal distribution of the middle. We live with a non-terminal amount of each of these doubts about ourselves and instead of it being overtly obvious, it is a chronic underestimation of ourselves, of our abilities, and of what we deserve.

For those of us who experience a crippling amount of these conditions, we get help, either voluntarily or otherwise, because without it we do not function well within society. But most of us live with just enough to second-guess ourselves, lower our expectations, and accept mediocrity as the norm.

To live as our authentic selves we have to accept that we are fallible and, though we should always work to right our wrongs, we needn't serve a life sentence for every mistake or transgression we make. Or worse, punish ourselves based on the assessments of others.

The irony, though, is that we're all very willing to forgive and forget everyone but ourselves.

I know for myself I found a very messy catch-22 at play between my low self-esteem and my feelings of guilt, shame, and regret. My self-esteem made me believe I deserved to feel guilty, ashamed, and regretful and the feelings of guilt, shame, and regret held my self-esteem as low as reasonably achievable.

Breaking the cycle anywhere along the process is enough to release us from that prison.

Ultimately what ended the pattern for me was the recognition of what truly defined me as a person and that was more than just my actions, it included my values and needs. Once I accepted that I was, fundamentally, a good person I was able to differentiate between who I was and the things I had done.

I also recognized that not everything I have done in my life was 100% in alignment with my values and character. I had violated my own rules from time to time. Living in contrast with those values and my character was what initially eroded my self-esteem enough to allow me to feel the guilt, shame, and regret that led to more bad decisions.

I realized that I have done and said a lot of things out of fear and scarcity that I would not do or say today living in abundance and confidence. By accepting that the regretful things I have done in the past were not based in malice or hate I was able to forgive myself and ultimately love myself.

Happiness, contentment, and love are inside-out actions meaning there is nothing you can do on the outside that will create them. They must first be felt and believed so that each of your choices is aligned with them, then your reality will match your intentions.

If we carry guilt, shame, and regret inside of us we will make decisions based on what we believe we deserve and no amount of avoidance or denial will change those outcomes. We must face our traumas and only accept responsibility for our choices and their consequences. Many people erroneously carry the responsibility for the situation which can never be resolved.

Recognizing the limit of your responsibility and authority for a situation is a very important step in resolving past events. A lot of us carry a great deal of guilt and regret about situations that we, as children, were powerless to affect. We are punishing ourselves for things that literally were out of our control and weren't our fault.

We're going to talk about the internal struggle in a minute, but first, we have to address the external sources of these toxic traits. If you are prepared and committed to breaking the cycles that are limiting your life right now, then you need to be honest about the number and existence of toxic relationships in your life.

Even if the source of that toxicity is a family member or members (who somehow get immunity from society's rules), you need to accept that some of those relationships may need to be renegotiated, through boundary establishment and enforcement, or ended completely.

GUILT

Guilt is a feeling of regret or remorse for the outcome of an action or lack of action. Guilt may be from real or imagined transgressions and moral self-condemnation. It can also come from a sense that one has failed to live up to one's own ideals, principles, or moral code.

An essential ingredient to guilt is that you must believe you have done something "wrong." That means that your sense of guilt is heavily influenced by your morality and sense of right and wrong, justice, and fairness. Additionally, guilt requires that you feel responsible or at fault for the outcome.

I call guilt the "coulda," "woulda," "shoulda" script because it's all about the judgment of ourselves based on our interactions with the outside world. If you've wronged someone through action or inaction, you probably feel guilty about it and that can be a healthy response by compelling you to apologize and avoid repeat offenses.

On the contrary, you may do something that society deems wrong without feeling any guilt at all if it aligns with your sense of justness. For example, if you believe your neighbor is stealing your newspaper (wicked old reference, I know) then you may not feel any guilt at all when you accidentally receive their free sample of laundry detergent in the mail and keep it for yourself.

Either way, it's important to understand that guilt is a conditioned response. We learned how to feel guilty through coaching and manipulation by others. This means that depending on how frequently guilt was used as a control mechanism in your upbringing and who used it, you will have differing levels of and inclination to feel guilt.

If your particular culture, family, or religious upbringing consistently withheld praise or used guilt as a weapon, you are very likely to have feelings of chronic or excessive guilt. Those feelings will make you question your motivations and exaggerate feelings of inadequacy.

Although guilt can be a force and motivation for positive change in our lives, it's important to ensure that your motivations for change and improvement are based not on feelings of regret, but on a positive self-image of being the best version of yourself.

Conversely, if your only motivation is to compensate for past wrongdoings, the motivation will typically not last and any failures along the way will only feed the feelings of inadequacy. You will ultimately feel your guilt was justified and you will restart the cycle from the beginning, losing all progress.

Although most of the guilt we feel is reactionary, we can sometimes feel anticipatory guilt for actions we haven't yet taken, or actions we're avoiding. Again, sometimes these feelings can serve to keep us aligned to and acting in alignment with our values and morals, but when these feelings of guilt numb us into inaction, they can be destructive.

Feelings of guilt, especially centered on our parents and caregivers, can be associated with disappointing those people. Having their approval withheld because of our behavior or choices will lead to extended feelings of guilt. Even when the affection and approval is reinstated we will often continue to feel guilty for our misdeeds and chastise ourselves through acts of self-punishment.

Into adulthood, this can manifest as acceptance of subpar treatment or the suppression of our basic needs because we do not believe we deserve to satisfy them. Even if we live alone, unresolved feelings of guilt can cause us to make choices that limit our pleasure or achievement because those things are reserved for "good" people.

Self-sabotage is another common side effect of unresolved guilt, again seated in feelings of low self-esteem and self-worth. Combined with the residual effects of a fused family structure we will hold ourselves back or hold ourselves down so as not to be happier than we "deserve."

These psychological effects are often accompanied by physical symptoms as well. Prolonged feelings of unresolved guilt can cause insomnia, nausea, indigestion, muscle pain, headaches, and even involuntary or uncontrollable crying.

More commonly, though, the most destructive impact of unresolved guilt is how it affects our decision-making. As stated, if we do not feel worthy of love, happiness, or success because of guilt related to past behavior we are prone to make choices that align with that negative self-image.

Since our lives are a culmination of our choices, that guilt alone is sufficient to create a life of dissatisfaction, resentment, and misery. All because we did not have the tools to recognize and forgive our errors and violations.

Because of this, we will use our guilt to justify every short-coming in our lives as punishment for even the smallest trans-gression against ourselves or our morals. In some instances, the guilt is so ingrained that we will not only deny ourselves success but sabotage everything from our careers to our relationships as atonement.

And because it is so successful at modifying our own behavior, unchecked feelings of guilt can be turned outward and used as a weapon against others in our lives. A "guilt trip" is when we exaggerate the effects of someone else's misdeeds to our own benefit.

Regardless of the source or manifestation of our guilt, it is important to understand its source and weigh the guilt against our intent and true nature. Any mistake made in error or without intent must be easily recognized and forgiven. Blaming and punishing ourselves for hurting someone else unintentionally serves no one.

Carrying guilt for something we did before we knew any better or when we ourselves were hurt and not at our best must be weighed against our true identities and given proper perspective.

SHAME

Where guilt centers on feelings surrounding our actions, shame is subtly different in that it is usually centered on feelings surrounding our thoughts and feelings about ourselves and our associations. Shame is the internal judgment of our character and, unlike guilt, is often experienced in secret.

Shame also has the distinction of being "contagious." That is to say, when we feel embarrassed for something someone else like our sibling, parent, or partner has done we experience that as shame. The ability to feel regret for someone else's actions or opinions is universally experienced as a condition of humanity.

Since shame directly impacts our social status it is used as means of behavioral control across the world. Breaking cultural or group rules has a lasting and immediate effect on the group as a whole. Shame in this context is a double-edged sword in that our actions can bring shame on the group and the group's actions can bring shame on us by association.

Whereas guilt can be traced to a particular action or inaction, shame can literally be inherited based on where we were born, our parents' status, or our belief system. When social standards or moods change we can experience shame from an entirely unexpected place. What was perfectly acceptable yesterday can become a source of shame overnight.

Since shame is so directly associated with our self-worth we tend to avoid discussions of any feelings about or challenges to rules and expectations of the group. People whose individual feelings or opinions about a topic conflict with the established standards risk exile for the transgression.

In this way, shame can exist just for thinking or feeling in a way that is contrary to expectation. Early childhood trauma is a common source of shame because we have negative feelings about the experience, but have to keep the feelings secret for fear of violating the expectations of the group.

Without anyone to express these feelings of fear and violation to, and assuming the treatment is otherwise accepted, we internalize the feelings of disgust as having something wrong with us, not the abuse. This form of gaslighting can have long-term effects on our self-worth and relationships.

Whether we are consciously aware of the shame or not, these feelings can have residual effects on our ability to meet our core needs, maintain healthy self-care, and our outlook on the future. Deep-seated feelings of shame will certainly impact our ability to establish friendships, intimacy, and love. Negative feelings about ourselves can also manifest in addictive behaviors, narcissism, and even anger management issues.

Shame centers on who a person is, not on what they do so even high-achievers can feel shame based on a number of social or psychographic traits outside of their control. Shame, therefore, is more dangerous than guilt and is often linked to thoughts of self-harm including suicide.

Because shame is based on a characteristic within ourselves, it only takes one thing about ourselves to generate feelings of embarrassment and shame. Despite being healthy, fit, intelligent or any other number of wonderful achievements, a single source of shame can make us judge our entire identity as unworthy or "less than."

Shame exposes us (at least in our minds) and makes us feel vulnerable and strips us of our safety and security. As you may recall, this results in an instinctive survival reaction. In cases where the source of shame is fundamental to our identity, we find ourselves in a perpetual state of fear and insecurity.

This leads to heightened states of anxiety and depression, especially in adolescence when our personalities are not yet fully formed (lower confidence) and there is a higher expectation of conformance to rules and behaviors. Since so many experiences are new, we are easily swayed and embarrassed when we make social blunders.

PRO TIP: If you're not sure whether you're feeling shame or guilt, reflect on your self-talk. If you say things like, "Ug, I'm such a loser" it's most likely a feeling of shame and you need to reflect on what it is about yourself that's making you feel ashamed.

If instead, you say things to yourself like, "Ug, I made the whole team late" it's most likely a feeling of guilt that you negatively affected those around you through a specific action.

Regardless, addressing the root cause of your shame is paramount to your ability to treat yourself, and subsequently those around you, with love and respect. Feeling worthy is the first step in making choices that are in alignment with your values and needs.

The tricky part to shame, though, is that we often hide it from ourselves. We deflect and deny through anger or even humor in an attempt to spare ourselves the repeated embarrassment of being associated with the flaw.

Exploring and facing your shame is the only path forward. I know for myself my father's addiction and my mother's abuse were significant sources of shame that negatively affected my self-esteem and ability to interact with friends and family in a healthy way.

Where they may have felt guilt for their actions, I felt shame by association.

What gives shame so much power is the threat of exposure. Where our first experience with a particular source of shame may have been public, every day since has been a battle to keep the shame concealed and that is what has given it power over us. We believe that if our shame is exposed *everyone* will know about it and judge us accordingly so we can never relax or let our guard down. The invention and proliferation of social media platforms that allow people to share personal details and provide anonymity for those who want to comment on them have created especially toxic environments for shame and shaming.

EXERCISE 14

Apart from exposing your shame to the world, you can first assess it by admitting your shame to yourself. Write about it, in particular write about your first memory of ever feeling shame about that particular topic. If it was about your body or your culture or some way your family embarrassed you, write it out.

Leverage the context of time and experience to assess if that particular source of shame is still valid. I don't know about you, but I'm not a skinny 80 lb. kid anymore and being called "Charlie Brown" doesn't really have the same impact it used to.

If your shame is what's preventing you from living your best life you have to start accepting and embracing whatever it is about you that is causing the shame. I love the movie Kung Fu Panda because there is no better example of turning your shame (Po's fat) into a strength. Whether you have kids or not, if you want to learn how to embrace your shame, do yourself a favor and watch the movie.

Naming, accepting, and embracing your shame are steps enough to minimize it if not abolish it completely. Fundamentally, shame is internal and associated with a judgment of ourselves. If you can accept the unchangeable things about yourself or detach from the things that are not your fault you will make significant strides towards allowing yourself to be your authentic self.

REGRET

Regret is a feeling that is normally experienced in the process of decision-making after the result has occurred. It is the feeling of wishing you had chosen something different, or not done something altogether. Regret can be classified as either "healthy regret" or "unhealthy regret."

Regret is typically considered healthy when it leads to better future decision-making, refocusing of attention or effort, or the elimination of poor choices. Unhealthy regret, on the other hand, can lead to rumination, low self-esteem, and chronic stress.

It is quite common to experience low-level regret early in our lives since we make many small choices and our decision-making skills are still new and untested. Also, many of the choices we make early in life are minor and few have long-lasting impacts allowing us to release the regret fairly easily.

It's normal to feel regretful sometimes. It's a natural response and helps us learn from our mistakes and avoid them in the future. But when we experience persistent regret, it starts to impact our well-being and we need to consider methods to deal with and overcome the regret.

As we grow and our choices become more impactful, regret for poor decision-making becomes more intense as we feel like we're "running out of chances" or we notice a cycle of poor choices. Obviously, if we grow up in an environment that does not easily forgive mistakes or poor choices, our feelings of regret can intensify and become paralyzing. The regret will also be stronger if the event has a close relationship to your values and beliefs.

Reflect on how these feelings are impacting your life. If they are getting in the way of your daily functioning or causing problems at school or work, then this may be an unhealthy feeling of regret that needs to be addressed.

The biggest consequence of having an unhealthy amount of fear of regret is that we are afraid to make any decisions at all and instead defer our choices to someone else. And as the band Rush so eloquently lyricized, "If you choose not to decide, you still have made a choice."

Whether we make the choice for ourselves or not, we're stuck living with the consequences. Surrendering the power of choice in our lives for fear of regret is a key contributor to a loss of identity and purpose. Like it or not no one is better equipped or more invested in your future and happiness than you are.

There are two main strategies to reduce the fear of regret in our lives. Most obviously, making better choices can help quite a bit, but if you're still looking back at past mistakes you should address those first.

Carrying the burden of past mistakes can actually create a habit of poor choices since we feel solely responsible for our choices and attribute any mistakes to flawed character or intelligence.

The trick to ensuring our regret is healthy isn't in trying to make perfect decisions, that's impossible, but in accepting that mistakes are a normal part of life.

The first step is to identify the reasons for regret, such as worrying about what other people might think of you or feeling like you can't do anything about your mistake now. You probably don't need help remembering what you feel regret about, but being specific about the regret is an important step in overcoming and resolving the regret.

Regrets fall into one of these seven categories:

1. Unrealistic expectations
2. Failure to make a decision
3. Bad behavior
4. Loss of potential
5. Loss of status
6. Loss of relationships and love
7. Lost opportunities

If you are still carrying regret for past behaviors or decisions, you have probably become hyper-focused on the *feeling* of regret and haven't taken the time to evaluate the situation in a very long time.

Categorizing your regret will help you gain perspective on how or why you made the choice you made and now regret. The perspective of time can help you realize that you may very well have made the best and only choice available at the time.

Additionally, acknowledging the time that has passed since your choice will help you accept that you have more than made up for any past indiscretions or pain you may have caused. Forgiving yourself for a lapse of judgment or having hurt someone is essential. Remember that who you are is different from what you have done.

Finally, consider facing your fear and apologizing (where possible) for your bad decision. If that is no longer possible, consider other ways to offset your regret through acts of contrition that align with your core values and needs. In that way, you can use the energy of regret to fuel something positive.

ACCEPT. FORGIVE. ATONE.

But obviously, the best way to deal with feelings of regret is to avoid creating them altogether and to do that we need to make better decisions. It has been my experience that the majority of persistent regret experienced by my clients stems from having made choices that were in conflict with their own values and identity.

The most unhealthy ruminating thoughts and feelings of regret are created when we knowingly go against our own nature. Violating our own values makes us feel like we have no self-respect or quality. "I knew I shouldn't have done that."

At this point in the book, I've lost track of how many times I've said this, but as far as I'm concerned it can't be overstated: fear is the root of all bad behavior, and in this case, bad decisions. If you want to make better decisions you must make decisions based on abundance and values.

Making a choice based on trying to impress or please someone else will almost always result in regret. Additionally, deferring a decision to someone else for fear of making the wrong choice usually results in a different form of regret. Regardless of which type of regret you most commonly experience, the solution is the same: make your own values-based decisions.

Indecision is a mental state that we often find ourselves in when we're called to make a quick or complicated decision. It's important to understand what the consequences of indecision are and how they affect us and the people around us. Failure to make our own choices or at least weigh in on the decision results in us becoming victims of other peoples' will.

Since our lives are the result of our choices and decisions, our failure to make our own decisions results in a life we don't recognize, don't want, or don't enjoy. That same indecision or failure to act creates distrust, resentment, and ultimately withdrawal.

Avoidance is not good for our mental health as it has been shown that those who have an indecisive personality have a higher risk of depression, anxiety, and suicide. In some cases, the heightened anxiety might also lead to some form of substance abuse as a form of self-medication. Indecision can also be dangerous as it can pressure us into making rash decisions without thinking about the consequences to ourselves or others around us.

Avoiding all regrets is impossible, but there are ways to reduce the chance of feeling so guilty for your mistakes.

Firstly, be realistic with yourself about your capabilities and authority. Overestimating yourself is one way to overcommit and create opportunities for regret. Signing up for everything that comes across your plate is a sign that you are people-pleasing or seeking external approval. Revisit your values, needs, and boundaries and only commit to things that fit within your life *after* your responsibilities and self-care.

Secondly, trust your gut! Intuition is the highest form of intelligence, so stop ignoring it. Not every decision we make has to be argued in a court of law or requires reams of evidence. Sometimes something can just "feel" right or wrong. Trust that just because you can't put your finger on a specific reason doesn't mean you're wrong.

Also, accept that short-term choices to "keep the peace" in the moment are never worth the long-term damage. Choosing options that we know erode our self-esteem or self-respect not only create a ton of regrets but they create a downward spiral of doubt and compromise. If you're worried that choosing your values above what someone else expects may damage the relationship, it's a pretty safe bet that that's not a healthy or supportive relationship and it probably needs to end anyway.

The next thing I would tell you to do is to go easy on yourself. A lot of times many of us are still working on feeling guilt or regret or shame around not achieving a particular standard. And the reality is it was never our standard to begin with, it was a really unrealistic standard imposed on us by our parents, our boss, our sibling, or our spouse.

You really have to stop for a minute, and this is a big part of where your personal Identity & Purpose come into play around living a fulfilled life. It has to do with recognizing your own expectations and accepting your own standards.

So if you're feeling guilt and regret and shame around something that you did or something that you didn't do, for example, something you didn't achieve, stop for a second to think about how important that goal was to you. Was it actually more important for someone else and you feel guilty for not meeting their standards?

Taking on that guilt is a really dangerous thing to do and that's one of those ways that you'll get swept into a cycle of continually going over and over a situation and thinking you're not good enough, you should have tried harder, or maybe there was something else you could have done. Stop for a minute and don't just take a look at your action, but look at your action in the context of the expected standard. Did you set that standard or did someone else?

Lastly, in the same vein, I want to share with you that you have to accept that it is perfectly okay to protect yourself and to protect your own rights. So if you're feeling guilty or shameful about something that you did in your past, but you did that in an effort to protect yourself or to protect your rights or to protect your own values, you really have to stop for a second and give yourself a break because there is absolutely nothing wrong with every one of us having our own set of values and protecting those values by the choices that we make.

CONCLUSION & NEXT STEPS

*"Love is: allowing and supporting growth
wherever it leads."*

— Charles Browne

Let me start by saying, Thank You! Obviously, this book is useless and senseless without you so it's very fulfilling to me to have been able to contribute to your journey. Hopefully, you've got more questions to ask of yourself and of me by reading it, so let me remind you to join the Facebook Group, visit my website, or connect with me and the rest of the community in some way as soon as possible. This book and my coaching are 100% focused on taking action within the context of *your* life.

I will be very honest with you and tell you that I resisted writing this book for a very long time because of my experience with self-help books and coaching programs. The truth is that in order to write a book like this I've had to write in generalities and speculate, based on the hundreds of clients I've served, on what your *most common issues might be*.

And the reality is that I have shunned a lot of other coaches because their programs were so general and did not consider, even for a second, the context of my life and my circumstances. Most of the time I came away confused and frustrated, filled with a ton of confirmation bias that I was, in fact, the problem and that I was never going to be able to be happy.

I know (I hope!) you have questions and gaps because that supports my argument that we are all unique and capable of finding our specific formula for happiness and fulfillment in this world. If a ~195-page book could capture every possible combination of challenges and doubts, what a boring world it would be.

If you still have doubts and concerns, that's a good sign! It means you're thinking for yourself and there's hope for you still! Reach out, find a group or a coach and get specific. But never give up on your true identity and your emotional needs; always let those guide you along your journey no matter where it takes you.

This brings me to my final-final point and that is: *Do not become addicted to self-help books, podcasts, videos, apps, or whatever as a way to avoid taking action!*

There are a lot of "gurus" out there who know that if you've bought any self-help materials in the past you are extremely likely to do so again in the future. They're counting on you not making any lasting changes and repeating this cycle as often as possible for as long as possible. This happens because we all get a sense of relief and comfort in reading stuff like this and then simply nodding along.

I know it's a few pages back, but I told you that knowledge is *not* the barrier. Knowledge is not the gap. Knowledge is not a limitation. Fear is, and no amount of knowledge in the world can overcome fear without confirmation through action.

Changing your life requires action, so take action! I know that can be scary, risky, and maybe today you don't feel like you possess the courage or confidence to change any of your circumstances, but I'm also going to tell you that in order to change your life you don't have to completely flip it over on its head.

In fact, I would seriously caution you against making too many changes at once. If you change your job, city, diet, exercise routine, friends, vitamins, pets, whatever else you think is contributing to your misery and then you actually feel happier, which change was it?

You have no way of knowing which of those changes had an effect, if any, never mind how to sustain that happiness or improvement. Before you can feel confident that changing X will result in feeling Y, you have to test little things, one at a time.

Make changes yes but do so in a controlled and purposeful manner like creating a healthy self-care routine. Blasting your life with 100 new things at once is the sign of a desperate, confused, scared, and hectic mind. Don't do it. Only make changes that you are confident are going to bring you more in alignment with your values and needs.

Sometimes you are going to have to create that change, other times that change is going to present itself to you as a boundary violation or a noncooperative relationship. Don't panic, don't freak out, follow the guidance in this book or within the Pursuit of Identity & Purpose community and make the choice that's right for you and your future.

The number one defense against poor decision-making in knowledge-based space (knowledge-based: high attention/focus, low familiarity) is collaboration! So when you're considering starting something new, get help, get a second opinion, talk it through, but never lose sight of the fact that you are responsible for your choices and honoring your values and needs.

Significant, sustainable change like this only happens from the inside out. And the very beginning of change starts with belief. Believe you are worth the effort because I believe you are.

Cheers!

ABOUT THE AUTHOR

Charles Browne is a certified Peak Performance and No More Mr. Nice Guy coach who specializes in helping the lost and frustrated discover their identity and purpose. He's also a senior nuclear reactor operator, project management professional, Lean/Six Sigma master black belt, submarine warfare veteran, open water rescue swimmer, adventurer, obstacle course enthusiast, lifelong martial artist, and serial entrepreneur.

If you think he's done it all...think again. In his own words, "I'm just getting started." It took Charles a hell of a long time and plenty of trial and error to discover his true identity and purpose, which—if you ask him—make up the foundation of a great life. Now, he's wholeheartedly dedicated to helping you do the same.

If you're feeling hopelessly lost and frustrated, if you're stuck in the mire of mediocrity, if you consistently fail to stand up for your values…you're in the right place. After years of personal discovery and professional coaching work, Charles has developed a tried-and-true way to help you discover your identity and purpose, so you can create the life you deserve.

Charles resides in New Mexico, The Land of Enchantment, where he writes nonfiction books and coaches his clients on how to become and live as the best versions of themselves while helping overthinkers and self-sabotagers navigate the tricky waters of creating a life that aligns with their authentic identity and purpose.

www.therealcharlesbrowne.com

WOULD YOU DO ME A FAVOR?

Did you love this book? Don't forget to leave a review!

Every review matters, and it matters *a lot!*

Head over to Amazon or wherever you purchased this book to

leave an honest review for me.

I thank you endlessly.

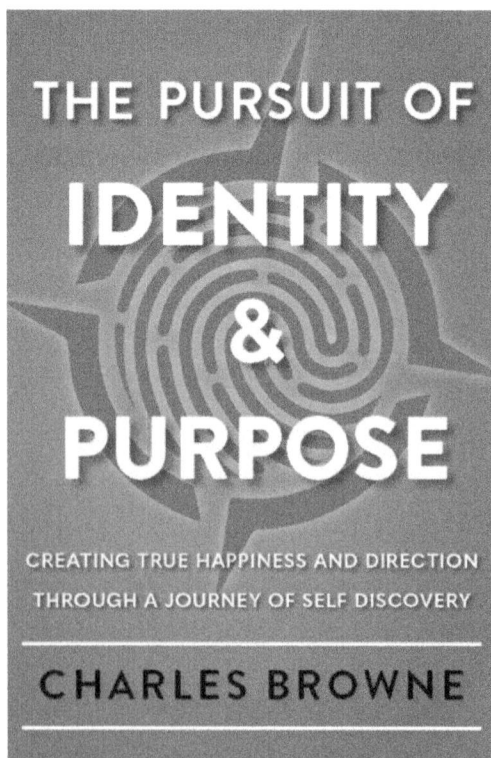

THE PURSUIT OF
IDENTITY
&
PURPOSE

CREATING TRUE HAPPINESS AND DIRECTION
THROUGH A JOURNEY OF SELF DISCOVERY

CHARLES BROWNE

Made in United States
North Haven, CT
10 January 2022